THE TENOR'S SON

THE TENOR'S SON

MY DAYS WITH PAVAROTTI

BY CANDIDO BONVICINI

St. Martin's Press
New York

Photo credits:
Pavarotti Archives, Modena; Photo Paolo Ferrari, Bologna;
Capri Club Operatic Archives; Modena Communal Theatre Archives;
Leone Magiera Archives, Bologna; Photo Alessandro Iotti, Modena;
Rex Features; Decca/Vivianne Purdom & Gianni Di Ludovico.

Additional text (page 183–202) by Constance Novis.

Every effort has been made to trace the copyright holders
of the photographs in this book but one or two were
unreachable. We would be grateful if the photographers
concerned would contact us.

Certain quotations that appear in this book previously appeared in
Pavarotti: My Own Story by Luciano Pavarotti & William Wright
(Doubleday & Company Inc, New York, 1981)
and from interviews recently undertaken by Nicholas Soames
(various publications), Mel Cooper and Michael Owen
(*Opera Review*) and Linda Marx (*Daily Mail*).

Library of Congress Cataloging-in-Publication Data

Bonvicini, Candido.
The tenor's son : my days with Pavarotti / Candido Bonvicini.
p.   cm.
ISBN 0-312-09920-7
1. Pavarotti, Luciano.   2. Tenors (Singers)—Biography.
I. Title.
ML420.P35B68   1993
782.1′092—dc20   [B]   93-26708   CIP   MN

First published in Italy by Editalia-Edizioni d'Italia S.p.A. English translation by Michael Moore first published in Great Britain by Omnibus Press under the title *My Friend Pavarotti*.

First U.S. Edition: November 1993
10 9 8 7 6 5 4 3 2 1

CONTENTS

THE TENOR'S
SON

LUCIANO PAVAROTTI

THE TENOR'S SON

He may be the most famous Italian in the world, but in Modena he is still "the tenor's son". It is probably true wherever you go that no one is a prophet in his own country, but this holds especially true in Modena. Before erecting a monument to Tassoni, the author of the most beautiful mock epic in Italian literature, the *Secchia Rapita*, the people of Modena took two hundred years to mull over the idea. Another of the town's famous residents, Enzo Ferrari, founder of the automobile company, always lived in splendid isolation: the only person he spoke to was his barber, Antonio.

What is Pavarotti's relationship with the people of Modena? One of mutual love, but a love that is restrained, muted. Though he never achieved celebrity, Pavarotti's father is first in their hearts. Fernando Pavarotti, a former baker, singer in the chorus, and critically acclaimed *bella voce*, beautiful voice, was never able to master the nerves that kept him from becoming an important singer, and for that reason, the people of Modena never had to share his voice with others - the crowds that worship his almost deified son.

Luciano brought his father into the limelight when the die had already been cast for both: the son was world famous, the father comfortably settled into his life in the town. Fernando still belonged completely to the people of Modena, and when Luciano forced him onto a stage, outside the city walls, convincing him to sing the part of Parpignol in *La Bohème*, the former baker and his whole city experienced a kind of shock.

Jealously proud of Pavarotti, the people of Modena regret not having been the first to applaud his voice for two reasons. Firstly, his début took place in Reggio Emilia, a city that Modena, a former duchy, has long considered *a dépendance*. Its inhabitants are mockingly dubbed *arzan da la testa quadra*, square-headed Reggiani. Secondly, he was first hailed as a great star in New York, and the key performances in his career were in the great theatres of the world. The Modenese people's conflicting feelings of pride and jealousy are easy to understand.

This love/hate relationship left Pavarotti like Hamlet, as if the recognition begrudgingly accorded him had brought some existential doubts with it. However, he almost certainly feels indebted to the people of Modena, and they to him. For ultimately Pavarotti has conserved a unique simplicity that would be the dream of any public relations agent.

Welcomed with open arms by world leaders, friend to the most famous celebrities, Pavarotti has never put on the airs of a star. In the many conversations I have had with him, I have sensed that Luciano is perennially unconscious of his celebrity: everything seems natural to him.

One key to understanding his attitude can be found in the acknowledgement he wrote in a book compiled by the music critic Rodolfo Celletti: "My thanks to all my friends, many of whom I have known since childhood, who have received pleasure and joy from my singing, and who have supported me all the way, wishing me all the best."

Much of the "Pavarotti myth" can be understood from these few simple lines. Pavarotti is beloved not only because of his voice, but also because he has remained down to earth. For example, his name is still listed in the Modena telephone book, so anyone can phone his home at any time of the day or night. I cannot think of any other Italian celebrity who has not become ex-directory. While small-town players pester the phone company to change their number every three months, Pavarotti has had the same phone number for many years. In any event, the people of Modena hardly think that they need to phone him to ask for autographs, appointments, or help ("He's one of us, seeing him is no problem," they say). If some outsider shows up looking for him or his wife Adua (who is his general manager, protector, watchdog, archivist, impresario and administrator) he might never realise that reaching Pavarotti is the easiest thing in the world. All you have to do is look him up in the phone book. Impresarios and journalists from other cities or countries follow the most twisted routes in their endeavours to contact Pavarotti, all to obtain access to a man whose telephone number is available to all.

The tenor's namesake can tell you something about this. Not only does he have the same name, but he lives on the same street, via Giardini, and is a driving instructor who taught Adua Pavarotti how to drive. Many phone calls meant for Pavarotti the tenor end up at Pavarotti the driving instructor's house. I wanted to ask him about all the bother his name has caused him, but I never got the interview. The third time I asked, he answered me firmly, almost rudely: "You have convinced me that sooner or later I am going to have to list our phone number under my wife's name."

I want to say as little as possible about my own friendship with Pavarotti (we grew up together, and I, too, have that typically Modenese reserve that so many people misunderstand). But I enjoy remembering that when I became editor-in-chief of the *Nuova Gazzetta di Modena*, after having been a correspondent for other newspapers, Piero Ottone, the chairman of our publishing company, came up to me after he had attended a dinner for VIPs in Milan, and exclaimed, "But you are a great friend of Pavarotti's!" The look of amazement in his normally cool and aloof eyes amused me tremendously. "We are both from Modena, and have been friends since school days," I said. Astonished, Ottone told me: "Last night at dinner when I said, 'Bonvicini is our editor-in-chief in Modena,' Pavarotti answered, 'Ah Candido! My friend Candido'." This was the only time I ever felt that Ottone regarded me as an equal; thereafter, he quickly withdrew into the role of the distant superior.

A WORSHIPPER
OF WOMEN

An American music critic, Rodolfo Celletti, said of Pavarotti, "When he was born, God kissed his vocal cords."

When Celletti reminded him of this, Pavarotti replied: "When as a boy I used to sing in the courtyard at home, many of our neighbours protested, shouting at me to stop. I am not at all convinced that I was born with an exceptional voice."

Thus Pavarotti had his début amid the protests of an apartment building on the outskirts of Modena, and he credits neither God nor his parents with having given him his voice. Rather he admits to having built his voice little by little through hard work. In order to understand this, two things must be kept in mind: he is a rigorous professional, and he is an inflexible judge of himself.

In a world populated by shadowy, flighty, vulgar stars, who are insensitive to all feeling and dominated by egocentric, greedy managers, Pavarotti owes his uniqueness partly to a happy and peaceful childhood, filled with friends and a large family that lived in post-agrarian simplicity. A peaceful existence with no room for illusions or wild dreams.

In 1935, the year Pavarotti was born, Modena had 110,000 inhabitants. Its borders stretched as far as the first ancient houses of the ducal city. The landscape was still inhabitable, filled with fields and trees. Luciano's father was a baker. His mother worked in a cigar factory. By a unique coincidence, the soprano Mirella Freni was born at almost the same time in another house in Modena. Luciano entered life like a hereditary prince. With the exception of Fernando, his father, his childhood universe was populated exclusively by women and confined to only a few rooms. Little Luciano slept in his parents' bed for five years, until his little sister Gabriella arrived. He then slept on a foldaway bed that was pulled out at night and folded back up in the morning.

In the autobiography he wrote with the American journalist William Wright (*Pavarotti: My Own Story*, Doubleday & Company Inc, 1981), Pavarotti said, "If I could find that iron bed now, I would pay its weight in gold; it would bring back so much."

Everyone has observed that Luciano worships women. No wonder: he spent his childhood surrounded by women. The centre of his life was his grandmother Giulia: "A wonderful woman. I adored her," he says. When he was born he was named Luciano because Signora Giulia had just lost her daughter, Lucia.

But if his grandmother always had the first and last word at home, Luciano was the true centre of attention, doted on by two aunts. Celletti was right to point out that these circumstances are relevant to the "particular tenorism of Pavarotti, who sees the tenor first and foremost as a man whose voice expresses worship, as well as love, for an idealised female figure."

But what was Pavarotti's childhood like? In his own words: "I never thought of us as rich or poor. We always had enough. We never had a car and we didn't have a radio until long after most other people had them. My father's little motorbike was the family transportation. I never thought about what we didn't have; I am still that way. All around me I see people making themselves unhappy with such thoughts."

Playing sports long and hard was also good for him: "I didn't think about the future. What child does? I just lived every day as it came, and the days were beautiful."

His mother Adele claims that she predicted a glorious future for Luciano, and that when he was born his crying caused both she and the doctor to remark "che acuti!" what high notes!

He grew up playing peacefully, but with no holds barred, convinced that the world was contained in the five-hundred-yard radius around his family house; going beyond that was of no interest to Pavarotti or his friends. There were daydreams, of course: daydreams that filled the same role as fairy tales.

When one of his father's friends, a worker in a factory that made aeroplane parts, sat him on his knee and assured him that they would build a real aeroplane together, the little boy's imagination thrived on this dream until he was nine years old. Then he abandoned the project, without crying over it.

In fact, it was to Celletti that Pavarotti declared, "Never again will I sing the part of an evil tenor," after having sung Tebaldo in Bellini's opera _I Capuleti e i Montecchi_, The Capulets and the Montagues, at La Scala in 1966. Pavarotti was still not Pavarotti then, but he already had clear ideas, even about what he should turn down. He was fully capable of declining an engagement, and missing a potentially important turning point in his career, in order not to deny his way of being and thinking.

Why does Pavarotti sing? What are the roots of his career? His father lived for the family, work and opera. Recordings of the great singers filled their evenings at home, with the voices of Schipa, Caruso and Martinelli being played one after the other, over and over again.

Growing up, opera so absorbed the boy that his first stage was the courtyard of the apartment building, and his first garlands were the sweets and chocolates his neighbours threw down to him, provided he didn't decide to perform too early in the morning or late at night. Perhaps it was then that Pavarotti, after his day-dreaming about building an aeroplane, began little by little to dream of becoming a singer.

At the age of eight Luciano had to leave Modena. Italy was

torn by war, and Modena, an industrial city, was a strategic target. The Pavarotti family took refuge at a farmer's house outside the small village of Gargallo, near Carpi. Fernando Pavarotti was able to stay out of the fighting because he was a baker, and bread was almost the only food left for the exhausted and disheartened populace. The profession "baker" on his papers became the magic password allowing Fernando through all the checkpoints. But one evening he ran into an inflexible officer and ended up in jail. In the Pavarotti home those were terrifying hours, distraught days. Pleas with the Germans were of no use. The baker was a mild-mannered man who thought only of his oven, but those were days when everyone was under suspicion.

When the time came to select those who were to be sent to certain death, the task was given to the fascists. The order was given to send everyone to the concentration camps, but Fernando's good bread had made a strong impression on one official, and the baker was sent home.

Meanwhile, Luciano worked in the fields and sang his head off. When the war ended the family returned home. In the evenings, the baker would take his nine-year-old son by the hand and the two would sing vespers together in the church choir. The boy's first chance to sing a solo came when the boy soprano fell ill, and Luciano had to stand in for him. This was the first time Luciano would face the public by himself.

"The music," he remembers, "was too high for me. I almost strangled myself. It was the most horrible experience. If someone had told me then that I would spend my life singing high notes, I would have gone at him with my fists."

But it was only a slight detour. Young Luciano had already been bitten by the bug, and three years later, when he was twelve, he went to the Modena theatre to hear Beniamino Gigli. "His voice was familiar to me, my father's records of him were worn out from being played so much, I wanted to see him up close, and especially to hear him."

He followed Gigli's vocalising in ecstasy for an hour, then ran through the audience to throw himself into the singer's arms.

Gigli was the first to learn of Pavarotti's destiny. "When I grow up I'm going to be a tenor too," the boy told him. Gigli's response was affectionate, almost paternal. He whispered "Bravo," but added, "You will have to work hard, and realise that every time you sing, you start all over again; you never stop studying."

Focusing wide-eyed on Gigli, the little boy asked, "How long did you study?" Gigli replied, "You heard me studying now. I just finished, for today. I am still studying, do you understand?"

William Wright, who collected these anecdotes for Pavarotti's semi-autobiographical book, claims that this memory still moves the tenor. With his usual candour, Luciano admits: "I can't tell you what an impression that made on me. He was world-famous, acknowledged by everyone to be one of the great singers of all time; yet he was still working to improve his artistry, still studying. I think about that even now, and I hope I am the same, that I will always keep the desire to become better."

Pavarotti retains a kind of religious, mystical, commitment to his "work". And he insists on referring to it as "work", claiming: "You can always love your work; your profession, at best, you can exercise." Few people realise that the joyful tenor, the man who is always smiling, is almost a cloistered monk, an athlete in perpetual training for an important race, a world record-holder who is always trying to beat his own record.

Pavarotti has great respect for his voice, and recently has begun to respect his body too, and has gone on a diet. He discovered that an overly large physique could end up damaging his voice, and with total discipline he accepted a regimen that goes to cruel extremes. At Tabiano di Salsomaggiore, a thermal spa near Parma, they gave him the key to solving his problem without being devoured by hunger.

Before the nutritionists and dieticians were able to win him over, Pavarotti did not merely eat and drink: he devoured food and guzzled oceans of Coca-Cola and Lambrusco wine. I have had dinner at his house and witnessed his eating habits at first hand. He can be absolutely voracious. The speed with which the spaghetti and Coca-Cola disappeared into his mouth was fascinating and unsettling at the same time. Where was the romantic Rodolfo, the proud Radames? The man I saw was appetite personified!

Since Pavarotti has begun a more sensible approach to food, he seems rejuvenated. Which is more difficult - holding a note, or steering clear of a plate of spaghetti? Pavarotti refuses to answer, but bursts out laughing. Who knows what he's thinking?

He has also begun to protect his vocal cords very carefully, and the minute something is not in perfect order, he stops performing. There have been times in the past twenty years when some hasty reporters thought they could predict that Pavarotti would suffer a vocal crisis, but these prophets of bad tidings have regularly been proven wrong.

When Luciano Pavarotti cancels a performance he always does it for very sensible reasons. With his technique, there were many times when he could have sung even though he wasn't in top shape. But he knows that straining his voice will set a dangerous precedent, and could somehow compromise his future potential.

Beniamino Gigli's short lesson, learned at so young an age, has always guided Pavarotti, who is undoubtedly the creator, interpreter and protagonist of one of the greatest artistic enterprises. But each fortune he earns is built upon hardship and sacrifice, and the endless commitment of days put together without compromises, planned minute-by-minute, from the early hours of the morning to late at night.

PAVAROTTI'S
FEARS

I once asked Pavarotti: "What is fear?"

"Fear," he replies, with the sly grin he has when he knows he shouldn't take himself too seriously, "is, according to Montaigne, the thing which I fear."

Who said that opera singers are uneducated, and that tenors in particular are ignoramuses who do nothing more than worship their own vocal cords? Pavarotti, a high school graduate, has cultivated and profited from his humanistic education, and uses it wisely. However, if it weren't for the practical, peasant wisdom that has guided him and lies behind his education, and his eternal optimism, Pavarotti might fall prey to his fears or be poisoned by them. But he has always found an antidote to them, and he appears, on stage as in life, to be a paragon of courage - indeed he can even resemble a roaring lion, or a man-eating ogre. But he also has a tender heart, and his goodness generates optimism, and so fear is, by and large, defeated.

"But you always have to be at least a little afraid," says Pavarotti." A little fear is wise, keeping you away from temptation, from flattery to your ego, and leading you to think before you act and to avoid showing off."

"So then, could we say that *del diman non hai certezza*, no one knows what tomorrow will bring?"

"Enough with the famous quotations," smiles Pavarotti, "otherwise I'll come off looking erudite, the last thing I want. Not that I'm trying to pass myself off as uneducated; when I get the chance, I still read a good book. In Pesaro, when I'm on vacation, I devour books the way I used to devour a plate of spaghetti. But it is by thinking that I found the strength not to be afraid. And what conclusion did I reach? That even if fear can act as a good advisor, there is no use cultivating it. In the long run it can only hurt you. But if you use it as a pinch of salt in the soup of life, that's another matter.

"For example, while I was still a boy, I should have been frightened to death when a doctor considered me more dead than alive. He whispered to my parents, 'The child is bound for heaven'."

Pavarotti is referring to an incident that took place in 1947. The family was having dinner when twelve-year-old Luciano suddenly couldn't feel anything in his legs. They put him in bed with a high fever, and shortly thereafter he went into a coma. Pavarotti continues: "The doctor came running, and openly confessed that he could not tell what was wrong, but that it seemed to be some sort of blood disease. He prescribed penicillin, and thanks to my father I was one of the first to use it - since he was a baker, all doors were open for him. But the outlook was so bleak that my mother sobbed to a visitor worried about my health, 'There's not much we can do'. Everyone thought that I couldn't hear, but I picked up every word. You can imagine the psychological state I was in."

So they called the priest. The child was as still as a statue: dangerously ill and terrified.

"Since there was nothing more that could be done, the priest thought the best thing would be to prepare me for the great crossing. 'My boy', he told me, holding my hand, 'the moment has arrived to prepare yourself for a great happiness. It is your moment to go to heaven'. From what little I understood (I was in a semi-conscious state), I didn't think that was such a great moment. I enjoyed life, I loved running around with my friends, and I dreamed about Gigli and his voice. From the back of the room someone whispered gloomily, 'He won't live for another week'.

"I thought that death should be afraid of me, and it really was afraid. Now I can say it simply and maybe presumptuously, but then I felt as if I were caught in a terrible game, and I did everything I could to win."

He did recover, wondrously and inexplicably. As mysteriously as the disease had appeared, his good health returned, permanently. After seven days suspended between life and death, his fever suddenly disappeared, and many people have since claimed that his recovery was a modern miracle.

Today Pavarotti can say in a level-headed way, "I don't want to make this sound too dramatic, but the truth is that at the age of twelve, I looked death in the face." To William Wright he confided: "Such an encounter with my own death has made me value life enormously ever since. If I am allowed to be alive, then I want to be *alive*. I want to live life as fully as possible. Having seen what it is to die, I know that life is good - even life with much trouble. Even life where everything isn't exactly as we wish. So I am optimistic and enthusiastic and do everything I do with all my heart. I try to communicate this outlook in my singing."

Two years before he fell ill, little Luciano had his first horrible encounter with death. After the German retreat and the fall of fascism, Italy was almost in a state of civil war. Luciano would walk through the streets of Modena and see one dead body, then another, and another; the image of those massacred and abandoned bodies would never leave him. "Violence is against God; that day I decided that I would fight all violence."

Later in his life there was to be a third encounter. It was December 1975, and Pavarotti was full of the anticipation of Christmas, holiday cheer, and childhood memories. The aeroplane bringing him home was already in the sky over Milan, but through a technical fault it was unable to land. In the control tower at the airport the staff thought a disaster was about to happen. The *Corriere della sera* newspaper quickly dispatched their top reporter to the airport, and began to prepare a special edition at the printshop. The plane was going to have to make a crash landing. In the air Pavarotti made a vow to himself: "If I survive I will sing the *Te Deum* in Modena Cathedral with my father". The passengers' fear ran high, and death could have been very near. At the last minute the pilot pulled off a brilliant emergency landing. The airplane hit the runway with a thud, almost breaking in half, and the passengers had to disembark by sliding out of the emergency exits. When the tenor appeared at the door everyone on the ground burst into applause, echoed by the people who were still inside the plane. "He is the one who brought us luck!" they shouted. Pale and speechless, Pavarotti disembarked. He barely had the strength to murmur, "A miracle, a second miracle."

After that, the fear of flying would never leave him.

"Every time I fly, I have to commit an act of violence to myself; every time I have to convince myself again that the airplane is a part of my work that I cannot do without."

But since "you never know", Pavarotti takes precautions, and he combines a genuine, profound religious belief with just a pinch of superstition. For example, if he doesn't find a bent, rusty nail in the floorboards, he will not go on stage. Most of the time he finds one, but sometimes he doesn't. And so impresarios wisely see to it that an employee places the talisman somewhere where the tenor will find it. Pavarotti is well aware that the nail was put there especially for him, but once his superstitious needs have been quieted, the performance can begin.

Maria Teresa Maschio, who, in addition to being a poet, is also a dealer in wine and liquor, once saved a New York performance that was almost cancelled at the last minute because someone had forgotten the talisman. She is a little superstitious herself, and always carries a nail in her handbag. That night she generously lent it to the theatre, without letting Pavarotti know. But at the end of the recital she made sure that she got it back.

Rodolfo Celletti has also questioned Pavarotti about his fears and the following interview gave Pavarotti the chance to speak about singing and superstition. The tenor told him: "Every performance is an unknown, a kind of Russian roulette. This is the point. But even if you are afraid, controlling your nerves, if you can, will save you. If you cannot control your nerves, then you lack one of the indispensable elements for success. Singers gifted with splendid voices - better tenors than I am - have ended up in small parts or in the chorus because they could not control their nerves on stage. At the beginning, I was filled with a kind of fear different from what you feel in your dressing room. I was afraid that I would not be welcomed into the theatre world, that I would be relegated to the sidelines."

He explained to Celletti that early in his career he was terrified by the idea of entering into direct or indirect competition with colleagues who had been performing for some time. There were too many tenors whom he considered better than himself.

"How many tenors were you intimidated by?" Celletti asked him.

"At least fifteen".

"No - four, only four: Bergonzi, Corelli, Kraus and Tucker," Celletti said. "The others you are thinking of were already on the way out - their own fault, considering their style of singing. But in the land of the blind, the one-eyed man is king."

"Today," Pavarotti continued, "I suffer from a different fear, caused by a sense of responsibility. It's an obvious problem. Are you considered a good singer? Then you must do honour to your reputation."

"Don't you think the position you have attained could shield you?"

"I never think that. The stakes are too high."

Celletti asked him if a tenor's fears are different from those of other singers. Pavarotti replied that he did not think so, and Celletti explained that Franco Corelli, for example, identified his own fear with the distinction between a tenor and the other male voices. "We have two or three higher notes," Corelli said, "and when you present yourself to the public it is always with those two or three notes."

"Pavarotti," according to Celletti, "does not think about the high notes, even though he knows, from direct experience, that they can be decisive in a tenor's career."

Pavarotti maintains that the high note is an animal sound. "When I think about the high notes in my voice I don't think," he says. According to Celletti, this means that Luciano's high notes are automatic, as a result of his great technique. His only fear stems from his sense of responsibility.

Celletti reflected, "I have often thought that fear stimulates man's religiosity, and that technological progress is one of the causes of the dwindling religiosity of industrial countries. In earlier times, travel by land and by sea, no matter how short the trip, presented risks we cannot even imagine today. Famines, plagues and cholera decimated the population well into the nineteenth century, without any effective remedies. In those days, they prayed.

"Singing is one of the oldest professions. It is intertwined with witches' spells from the totemic age, in which you can trace the origins of vocal virtuosity. Vocalisation in the sacred Hebrew music required a skill that is in some ways professional. There were excellent singers, and voice schools in ancient Greece and Rome numbered high-quality singers and voice schools. Even the Emperor Nero - whom some historians have classified as a tenor, though he was probably closer to a baritone - was afraid of performing, despite the fawning admirers and sycophants so noisily organised around him. To preserve his small, dark voice, he took laxatives, abstained from harmful foods, and placed lead plates on his chest for long periods of time. The archaic fear of a person who practises this ancient profession explains why many singers are so religious."

"Not in general," Pavarotti objected. "You must tell the whole story. And the reason is not fear but gratitude. A voice capable of singing in the theatre is a rare gift. How many professional singers can there be in a country like Italy?"

"As many as there are bears in the Marsica or any other endangered species," Celletti quipped.

Pavarotti replied: "Pessimism makes man cynical. That is why I am an optimist. But even if there were two thousand voices that were perfect for a career, what would they represent in a country of fifty-seven million inhabitants? This is where we get the idea that the voice is a special gift from God, our gratitude, and our religiosity."

When Celletti brought up the lucky nail, Pavarotti explained, "It is the material expression of the idea that you need help."

Pavarotti easily reconciles the sacred and the profane, the temporal as a state of necessity and the eternal as a fundamental point of reference. He lives by believing and believes by living. His religiosity is full and complete, his values absolute. Part of the reason why people like Pavarotti so much is that he interprets the ideals of a time; if opera had not been invented he would never have found the ideal expression of himself.

Regarding Pavarotti's fears, one could say much more, but I think we should listen to Joan Sutherland. In an interview with the French magazine *Les Avants*, the soprano spoke with Pavarotti. "Luciano has been so sensible because he never had any difficulty saying no. When the managements have come to him and said, 'Don't you think this or that would be a terrific idea for you,' he says no. Then he will politely suggest something else. He usually gets his way. But if he doesn't get something he feels is right for him, he passes up the engagement entirely."

Pavarotti's friend Niki Lauda, the Austrian racing driver, on the verge of winning his third world championship in Japan, withdrew after he had been resuscitated from the flames of Nurburgring. The heavy rain, which had reduced visibility to zero, induced him to stop. Lauda explained to reporters, "Sometimes you need to have the courage to be afraid." Pavarotti remarked, "He did the right thing."

Pavarotti has faced difficult trials with courage, and has even feigned recklessness, but on more than one occasion he has confessed to me, "I am almost always afraid, but I'm not ashamed of it." Celletti claims that Pavarotti . . . "has an excellent ability to stay in the centre of the ring. But he has to pay for this too, with intelligence, humility, reflection and daily work."

His first teacher, Arrigo Pola, said, "From the beginning I never had any doubts about Luciano's future; I knew that he would become a great tenor."

A LOT OF LUCK, A
LOT OF SACRIFICES

L uck has been an important part of Pavarotti's life. "A lot
of luck, but a lot of sacrifices too. Either way, the Eternal
Father favoured me."
    For his début in the opera *La Bohème* at the Teatro
Municipale in Reggio Emilia on the evening of 29 April, 1961,
Pavarotti was lucky enough to begin his career presenting himself
to the critics by singing Rodolfo, one of his most congenial roles.

Puccini's opera also provided the occasion for us to renew our
friendship. As editor-in-chief of the paper *Il Resto del Carlino* in
Modena I waged a campaign for the staging of a completely
Modenese *Bohème*. Pavarotti and Mirella Freni were already at
the pinnacle of their careers, but the idea had originated a few
years earlier, the day I met Gianna Galli, a promising soprano. In
those days I was a reporter for the old *Gazzetta di Modena*, and
Gianna Galli asked me to help her with some archival research.
On the day she entered the newspaper office and climbed the
rickety stairs of the former newspaper's offices on via Falloppia,
the little building, which was settling into a dignified old age,
shook with a telluric shock. The clerks piled on top of each other
on the mezzanine landing, the printers stuck their heads out of

the shop and all of them let their eyes slowly wander from the singer's long black hair to her legs, which looked as if they had been drawn by Boccasile.

When I came up with the idea for a Modena staging of *La Bohème*, naturally the memory of Gianna Galli came back to me. I had no trouble picking out the performers for the opera. She would be Musetta, Mimì obviously had to be Mirella Freni, Rodolfo, Luciano Pavarotti, and Leone Magiera would conduct. I also thought about Fernando, Luciano's father, but he protested that he was too frightened by the idea, and turned down the role of Parpignol. It was hard enough for him to think about going on any stage, but the Modena stage gave him even worse jitters.

Once I had checked on each one's availability, I started to write in the *Carlino* that the Teatro Comunale and the mayor had to do everything in their power to make this project a reality. Little by little, the idea picked up support among the sceptical people of Modena. Finally on 29 December, 1967, the Modenese *Bohème* had its premier.

As the evening began, emotions ran high, and the tensions were so palpable you could almost touch them with your hand. I was as nervous as the performers: if the production was not perfect, then the *Carlino* and I would be blamed for the idea. The response to the overture was frosty, and from my box Magiera's baton looked like an icicle. Then the atmosphere thawed, and it was a triumph of applause, a shower of flowers. That evening we were all truly afraid, and this was the first and last time I became involved in an operatic event. Since then I am happy just to sit in the audience. It's much more comfortable.

LONELY HOURS
ON STAGE

Pavarotti always tries to be himself, with his friends and on stage, and he succeeds. The public loves him for his genuineness, for his inability to turn his back on life, however things may go. He has fears and enthusiasms that allow anyone to see him for what he is, with no mask or screen, because his love of living and singing overwhelms everything else.

But who was Pavarotti before he became Pavarotti? Many extraordinary stories have been told about baby Pavarotti, little Pavarotti, and Pavarotti the apprentice. Some are true. Others are the inventions of compulsive liars. Anyone who accuses him of having given himself body and soul to the mass media makes a huge mistake; Luciano Pavarotti could not have been anyone other than the person he is, given his complete open-mindedness. The fact that the press, television and public opinion have taken possession of him almost to the point of devouring him is another matter. But could the most famous Italian in the world today have meted himself out more sparingly? I think not. Anyone who travels with him, for example, talks about how Pavarotti is capable of signing hundreds of autographs because he wants to make everyone in the whole queue happy.

He says, "I have had so much from life, and they are happy with so little. So what if I get tired and my hands get swollen?" And more: "In the age of total communication is it possible to be any different? I have worked hard in my career, but I did not realise I would have to deal with such a total embrace. Should I say that I'm sorry, that I can't tolerate the people? Should I act like an untouchable legend? First of all I don't think I am a legend, and I don't want people to think that I live two yards above the ground. Ordinarily, I want to be like other people. When I go on stage, that's something else. Then I must always and only come to terms with myself. Those lonely hours belong to me and cannot be shared. To build a character, give him a voice and believable dimensions is a hard job that I try to accomplish to the best of my abilities."

This is Pavarotti's philosophy. But he is also an optimist. Where does his basic optimism come from?

A picture taken in 1955 can provide a good clue. It was taken in Llangollen in Wales; Pavarotti is at the centre. It is a picture of an event that filled the pages of the newspapers. A Modenese group, the relatively unknown Rossini Chorus, won first prize in an international competition, beating out all the other groups. Italy was flushed with national pride, and the whole city of Modena rejoiced for the team that represented the city.

Back then I was a reporter for the *Gazzetta di Modena*, and the editor-in-chief had given me the job of covering the Rossini chorus. In the picture Pavarotti is a tall, thin boy. Above the singers stands maestro Livio Borri, the director of the chorus, but the person who stands out the most is on the far right: Fernando, Pavarotti's father. The image documents Luciano Pavarotti's very first success. Look at his face, his smile. Of course his face is not as round as it is today, but the eyes and the smile are exactly the same. The same simplicity, the same openness.

After the long trip home, the train with the Rossini singers pulled into Modena on a warm summer afternoon. The station was filled with yellow and blue flags (the city colours), with Italian *tricolori*, and of course with the singers' families and friends. From the moment he stepped off the train, the triumph belonged to Livio Borri. Until then he had been considered an excellent church organist, playing for the main masses at the churches of San Bartolomeo and San Pietro. From that day on, Livio Borri became a local hero. He got off the train holding the winner's plaque high above his head like a chalice, and the singers and their friends immediately picked him up and carried him on their shoulders in triumph.

For once the people of Modena let themselves go in a display of jubilation. But this was not the victory of a single man, it was the affirmation of a group. Because many people shared the glory, the joy could be explicit and collective. Among the many were the baker and his son, but the reporters paid no particular attention to them. Pavarotti's star had not yet appeared on the horizon.

I went back to the large newsroom of the *Gazzetta di Modena*, where I was awaited by my colleagues. I overwhelmed everyone with my emotions and my enthusiasm, and then went to hand in my report to the editor-in-chief.

Marcello Morselli told me: "This is everyone's victory, the city's victory, but of course we have to dedicate space to maestro Livio Borri - a great director, a great baton." That afternoon who talked about Luciano Pavarotti? Who would ever have imagined that he would become the most famous voice in the world? Yet the same optimism evident in the 1955 Rossini Chorus victory photograph is still present in Luciano Pavarotti today.

Umberto Boeri, a doctor who now lives in the United States, remembers him this way: "As tall as he is now, but slender and strikingly handsome. Above all, he was capable of being a friend to all." Thirty years ago, both took evening strolls under the mythical *portici* or covered sidewalks of the college in Modena, a place where young people congregated and eyed each other in the days when going out with a girl began with a few shy glances. In those days Pavarotti must have broken a few hearts, and there are more than a few Modenese women who confess to having had a crush on that teenager. One of them, now happily married, confesses: "To have him I would have done wild things, I would have eloped with him - he had the same eyes as today, passionate and sweet at the same time, a dream."

His female admirers are convinced that his eyes also played an important part in Pavarotti's career. His colleagues, friends, music critics and anyone who has ever met him will also tell you that Luciano's handshake is an important indicator. Strong, affectionate, even brotherly, it covers your hand as if he had always known you.

In his scale of values Luciano Pavarotti places friendship first. If he wants to talk to a friend, he calls at any hour, forgetting time zones and shaking you out of bed in the wee hours. From New York or from the other side of the world, he can stay on the phone for half an hour, talking about a whole range of things, always ending, "Thank you, you've made me feel at home."

This refrain is often heard in conversations with Pavarotti: "To be at home, to feel at home, to be able to go home." There is always something patriarchal in his behaviour and in his gestures; his hands and arms move around, compelling, affectionate. He is a charming story-teller too. He can start far in the past and then tell you about the latest performance or encounter. He forgets nothing, and his gratitude is life-long.

A BEGINNING
SURROUNDED
BY DOUBTS

Pavarotti's story does not begin on stage. Luciano, or rather *Lucianone* (big Luciano), went to high school, where he was no wizard at Latin, but did well in mathematics, and even thought about going to college to become a science teacher. Toward the end of his time at high school he started thinking about the future, and he sat down for a long talk with his parents: should he be a tenor, a maths teacher or a physical education instructor? For a short while the scales seemed to be tipping toward the latter solution.

"I was agile, all muscles, a good athlete," Pavarotti recalls, "and that seemed like the right choice." But he would have had to go to Rome, where the Higher Institute of Physical Education was located, and pulling up roots is painful for someone from Modena. "So I thought about getting a degree in mathematics, but then we made a few calculations and I realised it would not be fair to burden my family's finances for too much longer. Should I attempt a career as a tenor? In that period," Luciano continued, "I thought a great deal; my father had confidence in me, but I was uncertain. What if I failed, what if I threw years of my life away for nothing? I came up with a compromise solution: I would try to become a good singer, but in the meantime I would earn a living by selling insurance."

And so in 1955 Luciano Pavarotti presented himself almost simultaneously to the tenor Arrigo Pola and to an insurance company. His voice and training made a strong impression on Pola, and at the agency they liked his commitment and dedication.

Before submitting himself to the judgement of Arrigo Pola, Luciano had already had many voice lessons with Mr and Mrs Dondi, who trained the most promising voices in Modena.

Standing in front of Pola's piano, Pavarotti sang 'Addio alla madre'. Pola would later say, "I realised that he had a perfect ear, and all the qualities to become a major figure." He decided to give Pavarotti lessons for free: "I was sure I was making a good investment."

But Pavarotti still had to make ends meet, and a very tough period began for him. He took lessons with Pola, worked part-time selling insurance, and also found the time to become a substitute teacher at an elementary school. His initial pay was five thousand lira a month, and the figure seemed like a dream to him. But the children he had to teach were a nightmare. Luciano himself confessed, "I didn't feel that I could exercise the necessary authority, and they took advantage of it." He told Wright, "They were absolutely wild, screaming all day . . . I wanted to kill every one of them."

Rodolfo Celletti comments on this period in Pavarotti's life: "Pavarotti taught in the morning and was an insurance agent in the afternoon. He was immediately successful at the second activity. I'm not surprised, for in addition to my music criticism and literature, I directed an agency and organised sales for almost forty years. Insurance agents are like salesmen; they have to get someone to buy something, someone who is unwilling to do so, and must therefore be persuaded. Pavarotti has all the characteristics of a great persuader. He never takes his eyes off the person he is speaking to, scrutinising and observing them like radar. He senses every negative thought before it is expressed. Then there's the smile, which he always uses well, his modulated and ingratiating voice, his clear, concise explanations, the winning joke, the perseverance and patience that characterise him during long interviews, and also his ability, whenever you try to pin him down with a tough question, to slip out of your hands, never to end up with his back against the wall."

Luciano Pavarotti proved to be adept at selling insurance policies: soon his monthly earnings were around twenty-five thousand lira, six times higher than what he was getting as a substitute teacher. Celletti adds: "For an insurance salesman, to persuade means to talk, and Pavarotti is an authentic persuader. But to persuade also means talking a great deal, and this tires the voice."

Luciano went back to meditating and thinking by himself and out loud with Fernando and his mother. Now the war of attrition began. Away with teaching, less time for insurance, harder work at Pola's lessons, and then the great decision: "I will be a singer." His teacher gave him enough confidence. His career as an insurance agent ended, and his life as a tenor began.

One of Pavarotti's favourite books is a classic by Baltasar Gracián, a seventeenth-century Spanish priest: *Prayer Book and the Art of Prudence*. Chapter fifty-five reads: "Knowing how to wait pre-supposes a great heart, and an even greater patience. Never hurry or be driven by your passions. If a person succeeds in mastering himself, he will also master other people. With the passage of time, you must know how to aim for the centre of the occasion. Prudent delay prepares successes and matures secrets. The crutch of time is of more avail and more efficient than the iron cudgel of Hercules. There is a famous saying: 'Time and I are enough for two'."

It is almost always said that Pavarotti was an overnight success, but a more untrue statement could not be made. Pavarotti built up his career with patience and perseverance, and his hesitation over the initial choices reveals a great deal about his character. It almost seems as if he wanted to put himself to the test, as someone preparing for the priesthood might do. He had the vocation for singing, but before embarking on his career Pavarotti tried other things until he made the big decision. There

is a saying, "A man without doubts is an idiot." Pavarotti cultivated his doubts until he realised that he could nurture and bring
out his inner securities. His entire career is a mixture of caution
and courage.

The early years of Pavarotti's career were spent performing at
small concerts. He sang without pay: he considered the refusal of
money a trial of sorts. His friendship with Mirella Freni goes
back to this period, and even today the two sing together
whenever they can. "There was never any jealousy between us,"
says Mirella, "and we have always helped each other: in the difficult moments, and there were a few, Luciano was a brother to
me, and I was a sister to him." She also underlines the uniqueness
of the relationship between Pavarotti and Modena. Recalling
that in the first years of his professional career, Luciano was
never invited to sing at the Teatro Comunale, she says: "That's
not how it was for me. Maybe they have something against
tenors. Modena is the most charming city, but many strange
things happen there that would be inconceivable in the rest of the
world. Maybe this is why he hasn't sung very much in Modena,
and this long-distance love affair has lasted. The people of
Modena are proud of him, he loves Modena and its people, but
that screen of reserve that can seem excessive won't go away.

"But the few times that Pavarotti has sung in his city he's
received great applause. His 1985 concert in Piazza Grande
caused traffic jams as far as the tollbooths on the motorway, and
kilometre upon kilometre of the entire central area around Piazza
Grande, a huge open-air theatre, was blocked for hours."

Freni confirms that success has not changed Pavarotti. "He
didn't let it go to his head; he's still the same boy he was when he
started. His heart is so big."

When William Wright went to visit Freni to put together the
book of Pavarotti's life, he found her affectionate, but worried. It
was 1980, and the soprano said, "I don't know whether all this
publicity about how great he is will hurt him. It depends on one's
nerves. I would be terrified. Every time you sing, it has to be an
incredible performance. Speaking for me, I wouldn't want it. But

if his nerves can take it, then I think it's terrific."

His nerves have not just taken it, they've held up magnificently. Many years have gone by, and Mirella can rest assured. Her friend Luciano still has steady nerves.

Few people realise that Luciano had already passed the crucial test in the mid-Seventies. He remembers becoming suddenly and inexplicably depressed. He was singing in the great theatres, fetching record fees, his private life was peaceful, but he was suddenly caught in an identity crisis that was difficult to fight because the reasons for it were unclear. But there was a reason: achieving success and overcoming the greatest obstacles had pushed him into a state well known by athletes: he was physically and psychologically fatigued.

Pavarotti recalls: "The only thing left for me to do was thank the Heavenly Father, jump up and down for joy, and instead I was filled with doubts. I thought, people applaud, but they never realise I have the same problems as everyone else. I was terrified by the idea of getting a single note wrong, I felt like a prisoner of my voice. I think that sometimes the voice can represent an almost unbearable burden. I was in conflict, imagining a future in which I would have to sing and sing until they drove me off the stage.

"Then I became obsessed with my weight. I woke up after nightmares about being fat, and sat up in bed wondering how I could be a credible Rodolfo. Who could imagine the romantic Rodolfo with all these extra pounds. I felt ridiculous. I was groping around in the dark.

"I wondered how I could get out of the tunnel, and thought that maybe I should see a doctor. I went back and forth between Modena and the United States. I was able to hide my depression from outsiders pretty well, but not from my friends and family. I felt like I was always on the edge of a cliff, and thought that the fall would be endless.

"And instead of a fall everything was solved after the dramatic landing of the aeroplane in Milan. That day I realised that I was wasting time, and that I was ruining my life. I decided to lose weight, and get back the smile I had lost."

STUDENT OF A
GREAT TEACHER

When Arrigo Pola decided in 1967 that he would never sing again, opera lost a major figure, but gained a great teacher, one of the few who has taught several generations what to do on stage. He has hundreds of students, many of whom have become important singers, and some who have been lost along the way. The most famous, Luciano Pavarotti, says "If it hadn't been for 'Arrigone', I would not be what I am today."

'Arrigone' made the great refusal when he was only forty-nine years old, the golden age for a tenor who, for that matter, was at the peak of his career, with the great theatres of the world bidding for his services.

"Maestro Pola, why the great refusal?" I once asked when we met to talk about Luciano.

"I had returned from a tour in Japan, I had done *Carmen* thirty times, and I wanted to spend some time with Margherita, my wife, and my daughters Anna Maria and Paola Rita. And I would have had to get back into Italian operatic circles. After having been abroad for so long, I realised when I returned that many things had changed, and that politics had infiltrated the stage. Some people even suggested I join a political party, any party. I felt that I didn't have to ask for anything from anyone, and I already had a strong vocation to teach. That's the whole story."

Today Arrigo Pola is an elderly gentleman with white hair: tall, vigorous and imposing. I sat in on one of his lessons. He was surrounded by a dozen students, and seemed like a patriarch to me. He knows everything about his charges; he doesn't just give voice lessons, but feels that a good teacher is also a father.

For Luciano Pavarotti he was more like an older brother. Luciano came to the same little building Pola still lives in, on the outskirts of Modena, via Siligardi 38, to ask him if he should give it a try. Arrigone immediately said yes, without hesitation. "I realised right away that I was dealing with a phenomenal voice."

"Pavarotti had already taken lessons with Mr and Mrs Dondi. Who directed him to you?"

"His father, of course. We were friends, and had studied together at the musical high school. Not many people know that when Fernando was younger, he thought seriously about a career in opera. Today he denies it, and claims that his true vocation has always been that crusty golden bread that comes out of his oven, and that singing has never been more than a hobby. The truth is different. When we were taking lessons with Maestra Mercedes Aicardi his commitment was total. Unfortunately, when the time came to choose, he felt that he would never have the courage to face the public. It's a shame, because he had a great voice. The fear only left him later in life, the day his son dragged him onto the stage in New York in 1980 and for his "Parpignol", which is really one of the best small parts in *La Bohème*."

Luciano Pavarotti went to Arrigo Pola when he was seventeen years old. "I taught him every day, Sundays included, for three years, except when I was on tour, naturally. Then, when I felt I had done my part, and to give continuity to his efforts, I introduced him to Maestro Ettore Campogalliani of Mantua. With him, Luciano continued with the training that would bring him great success."

"What kind of a student was Pavarotti?"

"When he came to me he was already quite determined. His vowels and arpeggios drove me crazy, but he had just enough voice, musicality and musical memory for me to realise he would go far. He was halfway there. I realised that together we would complete the circle."

Arrigo Pola's teaching principles can be summarised in one simple concept: music is mathematical, and specific rules must be obeyed. "I told Luciano what I tell all my pupils: if you don't have the willpower or the stamina, forget about it, otherwise we will both be wasting our time."

"Maestro Pola, what did you tell Pavarotti the first time he came to you?"

"That he would have to study from morning until night."

"And then did you check up on him?"

"I always do. I think that young people should be neither deluded nor deceived. I realised that Luciano would reach the top because he had rhythm, artistic intelligence, musical memory and perfect pitch."

"How would you describe yourself?"

"I am someone who has sung in half the world, who knows how difficult it is to make your way, and who decided to teach what he had learned."

Arrigo Pola sang on many stages, but what he remembers most fondly is his début at the Teatro Comunale in Modena, on June 20, 1945, in *Tosca*. He had sixty-two operas in his repertory, and sang in five languages. On the walls are pictures and many prizes including citations as artistic director of the Fuiwara Opera Company, professor at the conservatories of Verona, Bologna, Bolzano and Cagliari, and five honorary degrees for his artistic and cultural contributions, awarded by the universities of Tokyo, Manila, Miami and Boston.

"Which honour means the most to you?" I ask.

"The gratitude of my students. I still fondly remember the evening in Tokyo when I was awarded the Mask of Art, which is in a certain sense the Oscar of opera."

Under Pola's guidance Luciano Pavarotti grew, but there are other names on billboards half the world over: the tenors Giuseppe Morino, Vincenzo La Scola, Salvatore Ragonese, Ivano Costanzo, the basses Mario Luperi and Michele Pertusi, and the sopranos Maria Abajan and Michie Nakamaro. All of them are singers who have tread the boards of the stage of La Scala.

Arrigo Pola's students have won seventy-five national and international prizes - a record difficult to beat. They come from all over the world: when I went to talk to him about Luciano Pavarotti's beginnings, the soprano Antonella Manotti from Parma was hard at work vocalising. Pola felt she still had to fix the position of some sounds. Rather than teach her, he chiselled her voice, in search of a perfection that came out light and secure after ten minutes.

Then it was the turn of Canadian Manrico Biscotti. His father sent him to Arrigo Pola to learn everything there is to learn. Manrico's sisters are named Aïda and Gilda - opera as a way of life and not just an enthusiasm.

Pola makes his students sing in front of a mirror because the attitude is also important, and the voice must reach the public in the right way. The position of the lips is fundamental: "If the position of the lips is wrong, the colour of the voice changes, and is deformed," Pola explains.

Manrico does his vocalising patiently, and every so often Pola interrupts him. "Turn and open," he suggests, and Manrico, who is close to his début, does exactly what he says. Following Pola's instructions, he gives exactly the right vocal colour, or a different colour when needed.

Antonella Manotti is there with her husband. "Are you a singer too?" I ask him. "No," maestro Pola laughs, "that's all we need - one crazy per family is more than enough."

Arrigone bursts out with an infectious laugh. "Even Pavarotti isn't completely normal. His superstitions are wild: watch out if before going on stage he can't find a bent nail: everyone knows that story. Never mention Verdi's opera *La forza del destino*, The

Force of Destiny, which many people consider an unlucky opera. The baritone Leonard Warren once fell into the mystic gulf between violins and flutes, and the second time he dropped dead, struck by a heart attack. As if this wasn't enough, once while it was being performed during a cruise, the ship sank."

Maestro Pola, who does not believe in all this, stops and thinks for a second, and then, still smiling, he says, "Well if you really think about it, it's hardly an opera that leaves you feeling light-hearted. Everyone dies except the prompter and the conductor."

To his students, who have been following this little improvisation with amusement, I ask, "But does Pola ever lose his temper?"

"Pola never gets angry," they respond almost in chorus, "but if he starts tapping the floor with his foot insistently, we know we had better do our best."

Arrigo Pola has formed strong opinions of today's opera world. He criticises everyone: "Even retired singers from the chorus give voice lessons, the opera agencies are a mess, the politicians have ruined everything." Maestro Pola is in a position to say this and more. He has a good pension, after having taught at Italy's music schools for twenty years. He has dozens of students, but very few of them pay. "Those who want to learn something at all costs pay, even when they don't have the requisites to succeed. But they only pay for a short while, because sooner or later I manage to convince them that life doesn't end in a musical stave."

Pola is a teacher by vocation, because he thinks it is his duty to help others who have some future. Manrico and Antonella, like many others, come here regularly and he doesn't ask for a penny. His payment is when a pupil has a good début. He explains: "For a few years now I've been working even harder; I help them because to open the way they have to fight against politics, bribes, compromises, bad directors and terrible artistic directors." As he speaks, Arrigo Pola seems to lose his initial serenity. "If I don't have the courage to say what I think now that

I'm seventy, then I should shut up. When I started, when Pavarotti had his début, everything was different. The opera world
has changed. Mediocre foreign singers, and even some "greats,"
dictate their own rules, impose their singers on us, expect royal-
ties and steal work from our singers. We should reform the whole
business. Every opera house should have at least twenty singers
who could be understudies for the great performers, ready to go
on stage at the opportune time.

"Instead, businessmen oppress talent, suffocate voices and
destroy careers. They go looking for things they shouldn't pur-
sue, there's a growing megalomania, an interest in pomp and
uselessness. The whole opera world is rotting, and is in danger of
dying. More should be done to change it, before it's too late."

"We need people who can change the course of things," I
comment.

"One person who is trying to do that," says Pola, "is Pavarotti. He created a contest for young singers without recom-
mendations and political party memberships. Did you know that
some Italian singers go around with membership cards to three
or four parties in their pockets? With Pavarotti they won't get
anywhere, partly because they are so mediocre. But it's the truth.
When I started out everything was different. What great training
you used to get from Italy's provincial theatres. They were open
to young people so they could experiment, so they could learn
how hard it is to win over the audience and its applause. Today
we are flooded with foreign singers who are regularly imposed on
us, even if they have no talent. I could give you the names of
people who will only sing if they are accompanied by their court,
which they run like a stockyard. Too many interests have thrown
the opera world into disarray."

What happened to 'Arrigone'? This man is an angry tribune
casting ruthless accusations, who would tear away the veils so
that the curtain may continue to rise on fresh, young faces and
voices.

"Things will change," I try to tell him. "I hope so," he answers
with a sigh, "otherwise what am I doing with these kids?" His

students are leaving: one of them has an important concert in Parma, and his friends are going to cheer for him. 'Arrigone' accompanies them to the door. Six of them are trying to get into a Volkswagen Golf. He takes them by the arm: "Are you crazy? There'll be big trouble if the police catch you. Why don't you take my car, and bring it back to me tomorrow morning."

We go back into the crystal chandeliers and soft light of his studio to continue our conversation about Pavarotti.

"Who is Luciano?" I ask.

"A good person. Almost no one realises how many benefit concerts he gives, without putting a penny in his pocket. He is the most complete tenor of the past twenty years. Today there are three great tenors: Placido Domingo, José Carreras, and Pavarotti, but Pavarotti has the broadest repertoire. Vocally and technically he is unsurpassable. And he still knows how to judge himself, he has kept his humility, and knows that there is always something to learn."

"For example?"

"For example, last year I went to Boston to teach some lessons at the University, and I was happy because Luciano was also there for a concert at Symphony Hall. I hadn't seen him for some time, and I wanted to give him a hug. I had just checked into my hotel when he called me on the phone: 'You have to come right away!' I ran to the theatre. He was rehearsing a phrase from Stradella's '*Preghiera*', but he wasn't convinced that his interpretation was right. 'Arrigone, tell me how I can work this.' I made him repeat it, and then I did it: 'Why not try it this way?' Pavarotti gave it a shot, Arrigone applauded, and Pavarotti slapped him on the back. "*At pagherò anch stavolta* - I'll pay you this time too," he laughed, and went back to singing.

"Maestro Pola, how do you feel about your success, and that of your students?"

"Applause used to be important. When I quit, for a few years, I still missed it, it wouldn't go away. Then I overcame it, and threw myself into teaching. I'm very protective of my students. I never criticise them unjustly. Helping to create a beautiful voice gives me immense satisfaction."

"Maestro Pola, you are a tranquil, fulfilled man. Is there anything you are still afraid of?"

"I'm afraid that one day someone is going to pop up and say that you can teach with a computer, and it's already hard enough to make a living in a world where everything is upside down. Supposedly there are two thousand new methods of teaching. But the true teacher is still the vocalist, someone who can teach what the diaphragm is, and who can shape the voice properly. You have to fully understand that the voice can neither be photographed nor written. You have to know how to listen to it, trust your intuition, and then apply singing techniques according to the authentic nature of each single voice."

This is the lesson of Arrigo Pola, also known as 'Arrigone'. And at least one person learned it well - Luciano Pavarotti.

FIGHT TO BE
FRIENDS

Life is made up of small encounters: people who come and go, and when the time comes to take stock you realise that there were more passers-by than deep-rooted friendships. Henry Adams wrote, "You do not become friends, you are born friends." That's how it was for Pavarotti and Leone Magiera: same city, same generation, a meeting at the right age to be friends for life. By the age of nineteen Leone was already married to Mirella Fregni, and they lived in a house in the old part of Modena, on Rua del Muro. When both of them became famous, she would change her last name: Freni sounded better. They had a child, and though their paths divided twenty years later, they would still be united forever by their mutual respect and by their only daughter, Micaela. They christened her with this name in memory of Mirella's first triumph in Bizet's opera *Carmen*.

In my efforts to find out more about Pavarotti, I interviewed Magiera about his close association with the great tenor. The two are linked by a network of friendships that have distant origins: mothers, fathers, relatives who live almost elbow to elbow in the same city. Modena was still a small town, and one evening the eighteen-year-old Luciano Pavarotti sang 'Nessun dorma', on one of the first experimental telecasts of RAI, the Italian national television network. Leone Magiera, the son of a well-to-do engineer, was one of the few people in town to own a television set. The tenor's image could barely be seen amid the flurry of white dots that filled the screen, but his voice was clear as a bell.

"I still hadn't met Pavarotti. I'd only heard talk of him in passing, but I have to say that my first impression was good."

Leone Magiera had graduated from the Parma Conservatory. Everyone called him a child prodigy, and the teenager was fulfilling his promise.

The day after the "snowy" telecast, Leone received a telephone call from Adele Pavarotti: "Did you see my son? Would you be willing to hear him?" Naturally Magiera accepted, and the next day Luciano came knocking on his door. I asked him what was his reaction to Pavarotti's voice.

"It sounded beautiful and bright, but little."

"What do you mean by 'little'?"

"That is the way you would generally define a voice that doesn't have the necessary roundness and power, but which has all the characteristics to become an important voice."

Right away Luciano, Leone, and Mirella became friends - a trio that would unleash storms of applause in theatres all over the world.

"So you started off on a downbeat," I continued.

"On the contrary, it was upbeat. We worked together relentlessly, exchanging advice and insults. We were always trying to do better. Pavarotti, who was both teaching and selling insurance, already had a voice teacher. I was his first music teacher."

Magiera has had many accolades over the years from the greatest contemporary singers, whom he has conducted and accompanied on the piano: Franco Corelli, Katia Ricciarelli, Lucia Valentini Terrani, Raina Kabaivanska, Piero Cappuccili, Renato Bruson and Cecilia Gasdia. The critics have called him "the best Italian accompanist", and von Karajan wanted him by his side when he gave a master class on Italian opera at Salzburg. "Six hours of work a day: he set the guidelines, and I developed them. It was one of the fundamental moments in my life."

In concerts Pavarotti always insists on having him and only him at the keyboard, but for a while Leone was held back by his fear of flying. When he convinced himself that flying meant working at higher levels, Magiera got up his courage and climbed on board an aeroplane.

He got over his fear in 1985, when Pavarotti went to Beijing for *La Bohème*. Luciano and Lidia La Marca, Magiera's second wife, an obstetrician, almost carried him bodily on board a Boeing 747 at the Genoa airport. "It wasn't easy for me at all," tells Magiera. "I had stuffed myself with Valium, but I was anything but peaceful. And in fact no sooner had we sat down than the stewardess went to the microphone and announced: 'Due to technical difficulties passengers are kindly requested to de-board. Re-boarding will take place as soon as possible'. Amid the many moans, I was the only one who was happy. My trial by fire had been postponed, if only for a short while. I felt relieved, freed from a nightmare.

"We got off and immediately learned that an anonymous telephone call had been made to the airport: 'There is a bomb on the Boeing'. Not bad for my first time in the air. They scoured the plane from top to bottom and then asked us to reboard. You can imagine what it took me to sit down again. To say that I broke out in a cold sweat is putting it mildly." To reassure him, Pavarotti held Magiera's right hand in his hands, which are as big as the sails on a windmill, and Lidia took his left. Leone gave in to those affectionate squeezes like a baby. "I was even able to sleep for ten minutes. Not a bad average for an eighteen-hour flight," joked Magiera.

The flight from Genoa to Beijing was the beginning of a new life for Leone Magiera. He had already been the chorus master for Genoa, Catania and Bologna, the artistic director of La Scala, one of the heads of the Maggio Musicale Fiorentino, and of the Teatro Comunale of Bologna. After getting off the plane in

Beijing, he became a conductor of orchestras in half the world, and the sole, irreplaceable accompanist for Luciano Pavarotti.

Now that he has overcome his fear of flying Leone Magiera is proud to say: "I've now flown many times. I conduct orchestras and concerts all over the world."

I continue the interview: "Maestro Magiera, is it easy to work with Pavarotti?"

"Not at all. He is certainly not an easy personality, because he has a distinct musical personality. Sometimes he asks for things that you might not agree with, but if you want to collaborate with him, you almost always realise that he is right later on. Luciano has incredible musical intuition."

"Could you explain a little?"

"Pavarotti is a great interpreter. At times he may add a point to a score, but the results are always exceptional. Some great conductors have admitted that they often learned something from Pavarotti."

"You said that Pavarotti is difficult. Difficult in what sense?"

"He is very demanding in his work, he knows what he wants."

"Could you define his voice for me?"

"It is certainly one of the most complete voices in opera history, because his repertoire is broader than that of other great tenors. He went from the repertoire of the light lyric tenor to *lyric tenor*, to *spinto* (dramatic) tenor. He has sung Elvino in *La Sonnambula*, The Sleepwalker, Tonio in *La Figlia del Reggimento*, The Daughter of the Regiment, and Nemorino in *L'Elisir d'Amore*, The Elixir of Love. In his second stage, he was an unsurpassable interpreter of Rodolofo in *La Bohème*, Edgardo in *Lucia di Lammermoor*, Pinkerton in *Madama Butterfly*, Alfredo in *La Traviata*, The Fallen Woman, and Arturo in *I Puritani*, The Puritans. As a lyric tenor he was great as Riccardo in *Un Ballo in Maschera*, A Masked Ball, Fernando in *La Favorita*, The Favourite, Manrico in *Il Trovatore*, The Troubadour, Rodolfo in *Luisa Miller*, and Radames in *Aïda*. He has proven his immense vocal ability in some forty operas."

"Will he sing the title role in *Otello*?"

"I think he will do it sooner or later, even if in the early years of his career he stated that he would never be able to play a negative character. In his voice there is a vein of sweetness that will always be there. His voice exudes joyousness. The character of *Otello* has wild facets. Despite this, I think that one day Luciano can be Otello because this is one of the goals he has set for himself."

"Thinking about Pavarotti at the time of his début and Pavarotti today, how would you say he has changed musically?"

"Initially his strong point was his high notes; through the years his most important feature has become the interpretative force that makes him such a great singer of Verdi's repertoire."

"Are Pavarotti's smile and cordiality really genuine, authentic?"

"Basically they are, but for the last few years he has no longer enjoyed being surrounded by crowds. He prefers to study, and to stay in his hotel room. He has other goals in mind. However, he still knows how to offer the best of himself to the public. He was born under the sign of Libra - sometimes his behaviour wavers, then he finds the perfect balance again."

"Can you tell me about Pavarotti and dieting? One evening we ate at Baglioni's. He refused many tempting dishes, and settled for a filet. He seemed peaceful and determined."

"Luciano has always been sluggish in his relationship with the table, and he has to fight with himself to stay on a diet. It's true, he might choose a filet, but then he steals bits of food from the plates of other people he is dining with. He is as fast and clever as a cat. Luckily he almost always has inflexible guards nearby: his wife Adua, his daughters, and his secretaries Giovanna and Judith. Judith is a particularly tough health fanatic. But Luciano has been the cause of incredible scenes. He'll have a brutal fight with the *sommeliers* if they serve him lambrusco at room temperature. He wants it chilled, almost frozen, because he feels that lambrusco is a sparkling wine, and this is the way it should be drunk."

"Is he consistent in his attempts to cheat on his diet?"

"Lately you could say that Luciano has adjusted to becoming

more serious. At the beginning it was different. He promised that he wanted to lose weight, and would hole up in Uscio with the set-designer Piero Zuffi and with Romano Gandolfi, the conductor. They promised to keep a close watch on each other, and then, at night, they would escape by the window, go to the nearest restaurant, and stuff themselves like pigs. All three of them have about the same tonnage. Some people say that they went home arm in arm singing Disney's 'We are three little pigs, we are three little pigs, that nobody can divide'."

"Pavarotti is already a scout for new talent with the contest designed for young people. In the future, do you see Pavarotti as a teacher?"

"Yes, I think Pavarotti could be a wonderful teacher, but he will demand a lot from his students. When we went to Beijing with *La Bohème*, the poor guy who played Marcello made a wrong move, Luciano sent out a terrifying yell from the wings that crossed the stage and split the audience like a sword: *Imbezil*, Imbecile. Luckily no one in the Chinese audience knew what the word meant, nor did they know that almost inhuman shout came from Pavarotti's huge mouth."

"Pavarotti has recorded albums containing both arias and popular songs. Purists might have expected a less brazen combination. What do you think?"

"I think that Luciano was right to record those albums. There was a pressing demand, especially in the United States. Popularity also requires attention to the public's demands. In any case they are irreproachable interpretations."

"Maestro Magiera, have you and Pavarotti ever had a quarrel, a fight?"

"We are always fighting, we have been fighting ever since we met. Mirella, he, and I used to fight like cats and dogs at the beginning. But they were constructive quarrels. We wanted to make each other improve. I had one of the last, most dramatic fights in Dortmund. Luciano's angry voice sounded like thunder. Lidia got in the middle to calm us down, and then took him aside and asked if there wasn't anything he could do to restore peace between us. Pavarotti broke out in one of his laughs, 'What are you surprised at, we have always fought over musical questions, but the consequences have constantly been positive'."

"What was the reason for the disagreement?"

"We did not agree on what character to give the orchestral introduction to a *romanza* from *Lucia di Lammermoor*. We stubbornly argued whether Luciano should portray Edgardo as heroic or pathetic. I was for the first, Luciano was for the second. I screamed at him: "How can you be pathetic with all those trumpets blaring? You have to be heroic!" Luciano countered, "Edgardo must mainly appear saddened: he has been abandoned by the woman he loves, and feels that everything is leading to tragedy." In the end I let Luciano have his way. He had succeeded in convincing me that his interpretation was right."

"What is Luciano Pavarotti for you?"

"First and foremost a friend. Sometimes I forget that I'm accompanying a great tenor."

"Where would you place him in a rating?"

"I am against ratings, and I wouldn't want people to think I over-estimate him out of affection. But I really think that he's the number one of all time. Because of the modernity of his interpretations, and the importance he gives to the meaning of a word. Because he knows how to dig deep. His voice has nothing to fear in comparison to Beniamino Gigli's or Caruso's, even if we only know Caruso through early recordings."

THE RETURN OF
ULYSSES

The Pavarotti family lives in Saliceta San Giuliano, on the outskirts of Modena. Their house is behind via Giardini, the street where Enzo Ferrari and his drivers tested their first sports cars.

Pavarotti's villa is enveloped in silence. The trees in the garden are covered by a mantle of golden leaves, and workmen are unloading a piano for the 'maestro' from a lorry. The sky is dark, and you can smell a storm on its way. It seems to me like the right kind of day to take shelter in a confidential interview, one that can cause no problems. But this interview would end up causing me all sorts of problems: it is always a problem to interview a friend, and to interview the wife of a friend is twice the problem. You already know everything, or almost; you already know that the Pavarottis live a normal life, that there will not be any astounding revelations to bowl the reader over. You already know that no legend resides behind those gates, that you won't find heart-shaped swimming pools or golden faucets there. The door will not be opened by a liveried butler, but by Adua or one of the three daughters. You ring the bell and indeed there is no butler nor the semblance of a maid, but Adua herself, the 'sweet'

Adua as she has been dubbed by journalists the world over. She wears a beige silk blouse, a kilt and comfortable shoes.

We sit in Luciano's studio, she behind a beautiful eighteenth-century desk. Adua repeats what she had already said on the telephone. "So let's go ahead with this little chat, but what can I tell you that you don't already know?" Indeed, what can she tell me?

I hazard a provocation. "Are you really as sweet as everyone always says you are?"

"I try to be good, I think it's a duty, but sweet, not at all. Certainly with Luciano, my daughters, my parents, and his. But to be sweet today could even be dangerous; this is a ferocious world with fewer and fewer human spaces left in it. Then I have my moods, like anyone else, and it is true that not everything that glitters is gold. The life of an entertainer has its dusty, dull side, and how. And it isn't always as fascinating as some would say it is."

"Happy, then, but with reservations," I comment.

"I would say that I'm satisfied, fulfilled, but that nothing is easy. Life is always an uphill battle for everyone, and when you are on the mountain top, you realise that to go down even one step can be risky. Luciano has certainly gone far, but it was so hard for him and for those near him!"

"How was it in the early days?"

"Hard, even if Luciano was lucky enough to have Alessandro Ziliani as his first agent. He was a famous tenor in the 1930's who left the stage because he had too many engagements and set up a very well-run agency. Ziliani believed in Pavarotti immediately, after hearing him in the Reggio Emilia International Competition in 1961. But in the early years it was hard to get him engagements."

Here and in Pesaro, where the Pavarottis have a vacation home, we spent some lovely evenings; a plate of spaghetti prepared by Luciano, a pizza, and a lot of Coca-Cola. He wasn't on a diet yet. Nowadays things have changed. His visits home have become more rare and more brief. These are the years of triumph, tinged with nostalgia for more tranquil days.

The interview is really difficult. We try accompanying it with a glass of lambrusco.

"Who is Luciano Pavarotti? What kind of man is he? I mean at home, with the family, away from the stage, after the footlights have been switched off. Who is the Luciano-Ulysses of the constant hurried returns after the tours and the recordings? Who is Pavarotti the husband and father?"

"He is a man like many others who, fortunately, tries to stop playing the tenor when he is home. The demands of his work never completely end, and always influence him. Luckily we still fight: it's a good sign, it means that our relationship is working, that we have something to say to each other."

"What do you tell each other?"

"When necessary we tell each other to go fry."

"And with your daughters?"

"They're grown up and wish he could spend more time with them. So when he comes home, he finds them all around him and lets them pamper him like a big cat."

"If you were to do it over again, would you still marry him?"

"Of course I would, even if living with a tenor can be exhausting sometimes. There are always pleasant and unpleasant sides to everything. But you forget the unpleasant things quickly when you love each other."

And the Pavarottis really do love each other. They are a family as tightly closed and impenetrable as a fist.

"Luciano says, 'When I'm off stage I wish that everyone would forget me. I have my people, and that's enough'."

I tell Adua, "Let's think for a moment about all the articles written about him and about your family. Don't you get the impression they are all photocopies of each other?"

"It's not our fault if journalists have so little imagination."

"That's not quite the case. You created a stereotype and sealed yourself inside it. You reveal yourself, but only so much."

"That may very well be, but the truth is that nothing is so unique about our life. At any rate, what right does anyone have to go rummaging around in other people's lives?"

53

"That's the price you have to pay for being a celebrity."

"We don't barricade ourselves in, we just want a peaceful life. Making scandals out of everything is painful. I realise that the tabloids may be disappointed in us, but we can't make up love stories to boost their sales."

"Exactly. Why is there never any gossip on the Pavarottis? They've got good and bad to say about everyone, but you two are like stainless steel, always respected, almost boring. And yet you belong to the international jet set."

"Only in passing. We have friends everywhere, because Luciano can't live without friends, they are his oxygen. But to everyone his own home and place. I would say that we are very traditional, and therefore maybe a little boring, as you say. You have to be a little boring if you don't want to give up your privacy completely. We don't want to arouse curiosity. Luciano wants to sing well for as long as possible, I like playing the part of his wife, and even though thirty years ago I wasn't interested in opera, today I've become so involved with it that I've opened my own theatrical agency."

"So in addition to your diplomatic duties, you are now working as a manager."

Adua Pavarotti has the profile of a sphinx. And what if she weren't as sweet as the tabloid story-tellers claim? I will find out in a couple of hours, when we move to the office where she has a small team of workers at her command, on the phones and at the computer.

"You met in high school. I was in school with you, too."

"Yes, I was in the third year, he was in the second. He had lost a year during the war."

"And it was love."

"No, just friendship. He was a good-looking guy, and one of the few boys at the school. We went to a party together and he said, 'Would you like to go to the movies next Sunday?' I answered, 'Yes, if my cousin can come too'."

"Not exactly a thrilling beginning."

"He was disappointed, but he picked up when he saw me

arrive by myself. My cousin had come down with the flu. We went to see a Don Camillo film, and in the dark, at the Principe cinema, he held my hand."

"And you?"

"I let him know that mine was *una gelida manina*, a cold little hand. I didn't want to get carried away. I thought we were too young, and I've never been one to get all keyed up too easily."

"But he persisted."

"He kept after me politely, and we started to go out with each other, but it didn't last long, six or seven months. We fought too often, and we stopped seeing each other for a year. I would run into him at school sometimes. He was on another floor. He tried to date me again, and became more insistent. I kept telling him no, then we started going out with each other again. A story like many others."

"You were engaged for eight years, and got married on 30 September 1961 in the church of San Faustino. There's a photo from that day that catches Luciano signing the most important autograph of his life. You both look very moved, touched. Luciano even looks a little worried."

"The love that began so surreptitiously had grown stronger. I didn't think Luciano would become famous, but I knew he would go far. I encouraged him, and I wouldn't have been upset about it if he hadn't become a big success. The truth is that on our wedding day we were emotional and a little worried. The two of us together were not able to come up with a decent salary. After teaching in the school where Luciano had substituted, I took an office job and my small salary was what allowed us to get by with some dignity for the first two years. I worked until Cristina was born, our second child after Lorenza, and before Giuliana."

"By that time Luciano was becoming Pavarotti."

Adua confided her memories of that crucial period in Luciano's career to William Wright.

"There were some bad moments but there were some wonderful ones too. Once Luciano had been away for several weeks singing in a small opera company in Holland. The company had financial problems, so they didn't pay the singers until the very end of the run. Instead of getting little amounts of money every week, Luciano got one big pile of cash at the end.

"The day he arrived back in Modena, I was teaching at school. I got home that evening to find Luciano had taken the money and covered our bedroom with it. There were bills everywhere - over the bed, the chest of drawers, the chairs - he had even stuck money to the wall.

"Another particularly happy moment I remember was when he first got a definite offer from La Scala. Luciano had already sung at Covent Garden with terrific success as well as in other opera houses around Europe. For a long time he had been in touch with La Scala, but they either wanted him to understudy or take a role that he didn't feel was right for him to sing. This was very frustrating. Even though his career was going well, La Scala, especially for Italians, is in a class by itself.

"One day I was in our apartment and I heard Luciano calling me from outside, I looked out the window and saw him in the garden below. He was waving the Scala contract in one hand. It was famous for its pink colour and I would have recognised it from twice the distance. In the other hand he was holding a metal orange-juice squeezer. It was a silly gadget he had wanted for a long time but didn't think we could afford. Thanks to La Scala the Pavarottis had plenty of fresh orange juice from then on."

"That gift tells you a lot about who Pavarotti is," I say.

Adua replies, "Yes, above all else he is a simple man. He knows how to be happy with little, and I sincerely think that he would have been happy even if he had not become rich and famous.

"The house he chose is also significant. He was born in a big apartment building on via Giardini, built his first house a few metres away, and the second house not much further down.

"He is a Ulysses, always and everywhere. He always returns to his origins. He is very attached to his roots. He is also a person of extremely fixed habits. In every city that he visits he has one hotel, always the same one, and he expects, within limits, to have the same room. Often he prefers residences, even if they are not the most luxurious class, because he wants to take care of himself and have everything close to hand. He doesn't like depending on others. I told Wright that he doesn't want to ask where the lifts are: he wants to know."

"Can I ask about Luciano and his 'physical condition'?"

"He is demanding with himself, as he is with others. Ever since he reached the right weight for his height, he has become even stricter, even more complicated, because he wants to keep himself constantly under control. Since it is not easy to have a doctor within reach all the time, he bought a kit to take his blood pressure. He always carries it with him. It's his security blanket."

"What about Luciano and women?"

"Luciano's life is filled with women: his mother, his aunt, his grandmother, his daughters, and naturally, yours truly, Adua Veroni. He grew up in a female universe, and adores women. Sometimes I think he ended up giving himself up to this condition: women, always women. He may have thought, 'If this is my destiny, so be it'. Maybe he sees himself as the ancient patriarch who thinks he can influence a little matriarchal world, maybe he sees himself as a pasha with a harem all to himself. He's like Fellini: woman is a protagonist to love, and if necessary, to endure."

"Tell me about Luciano on stage, before and after."

"He's a perfectionist, inspecting everything, including the lights."

"What is his best quality?"

"His generosity. The word envy is not in his vocabulary."

"And his defect?"

"When he is on stage, or when he is about to go on a busy tour, he gets neurotic. No, excuse me, write 'a little nervous'."

"What are his hobbies?"

"Horses and *briscola*. He loves playing cards with the Cuoghi brothers, who are his closest friends, and who deserve credit for putting up with him, because Luciano always expects to beat them. He would do anything to win, even cheat, shamelessly. He used to like playing poker with José Carreras and Katia Ricciarelli, now he definitely prefers *briscola*."

"Does he love Modena?"

"He couldn't live anywhere else."

"Why does he leave his name in the phone book?"

"I've been wondering that myself."

"He's seriously traumatised the man with the same name, who also lives on via Giardini."

"Yes, he's certainly exasperated that man. He's an industrial expert who was also my teacher at driving school. One day his wife asked me, 'Couldn't you specify Luciano Pavarotti, *tenore?*'. I told her that would be ridiculous. And she suggested, 'At least write *Commendatore, maestro*'. I held my ground, and promised her that we would consider the possibility of removing our number from the phone book, and she rightly objected, 'Then the phone calls and requests for singing engagements for my husband the driving instructor would double'."

"How did it end up?"

"There was an easy solution. He wrote: Pavarotti, Luciano, industrial worker. But people still call him: 'You wouldn't happen to be the famous Luciano trying to confuse people who are looking for you?' "

"Aside from the telephone, are both you and Luciano available?"

"Too much."

"Luciano is in demand all over the world."

"Everyone wants him. For every two hundred no's there's one yes. He is booked for several years."

I put this idea to Adua: "Recently someone said that Pavarotti is the last great tenor, and the soprano Magda Oliviero added, 'Things are getting worse and worse, voices are lost, heroic tenors are disappearing, and there is a shortage of dramatic sopranos'. I don't know whether this is a case of genetic mutation, but this is the situation. And the critic Rodolfo Celletti sees an even bleaker situation: 'Today's tragedy is that tenors no longer know how to emit high notes, but only shrieks'."

"I think that's a slightly pessimistic evaluation, but there's an element of truth. It's getting harder and harder to find dramatic tenors who can sing roles in operas such as *Turandot, Trovatore, Ernani, Otello, Cavalleria* and *Pagliacci.* I told you that I suddenly fell in love with opera, and this is why I came up with the idea, together with Luciano, of doing whatever possible to bring out new talent."

"How many singers do you manage?"

"About seventy; many in Italy, others scattered in different parts of the world. When they pass the Pavarotti exam they can rest assured. I try to set up engagements, they try to be successful."

"Let's go back to the crisis described by Magda Oliviero."

"She's right when she talks about tenors: there aren't great voices among baritones or basses either. However, technique has become more refined, and stylistically speaking there have been improvements. The truth is that contemporary life has caused actual morphological changes. Comforts and habits have made men less competitive, and there is a lowering of quality in every sector. Maybe we'll end up looking for good tenors or basses among woodsmen."

"And how are we doing with female voices?"

"The crisis still hasn't emerged. There are great voices, especially in the United States, but the competition is fierce."

Adua speaks with the acumen of a manager. From the moment we stepped into her office, amid thousands of phone calls, she has revealed the sphinx's hidden face. No longer 'sweet,' but determined.

At the door to the house I ask, "Who is Adua Pavarotti?"

"A woman who is like any other working woman." Then she thinks for a second and adds, ironically, "A woman dedicated to hard work."

"So you would like to change something?"

"If there were only a few more hours in the day. In the evening there's still so much left to be done. I'm always fighting with time. I have to think of the painter, the bricklayer, the young singers I'm in charge of, and my daughters, naturally."

"And Luciano?"

"He sings alone, luckily."

She says good-bye quickly, giving me a very sweet smile.

"I have to run. I've been asked to appear at an event."

Adua Veroni goes back upstairs to become Adua Pavarotti once again, for a few more hours. It's true, her day never ends.

THE TENOR'S FATHER
VOCALISES

It is October, the month for weddings. In the little house Luciano gave his parents, Signor Fernando, formerly a baker and forever a lyric tenor, complains to his wife Adele. He is afraid he won't be able to sing at the wedding of a couple from the mountains near Modena the following day. Moreover, Fernando, a great *bocce* player, is expected at a high-level tournament in Formigione the same day.

Pavarotti *padre* is still shaky from a bout of pharyngitis, and gives up quickly. "If I don't sing tomorrow I won't have to until next Sunday, but I should give it a try. What do you say? Let's see how this damn throat of mine is doing." His wife, Signora Adele, says reassuringly, "You just have a bit of a cold, it'll go away." I say, "Signor Fernando, let's give it a try, I mean, why don't you try? I will be a tough critic."

Pavarotti senior goes to the harmonium and begins to vocalise: "Aaaaaah, aaaaoh, eeeeeah . . ." His voice comes out clean and round. "It's a beautiful Pavarottian voice," I reassure him. "It sounds fine to me." Signor Fernando looks at me with benevolent scepticism, and Signora Adele scrutinises me with anxious eyes. They finally let themselves be convinced that I'm sincere.

Ever since Pavarotti senior stopped working as a baker, he has felt the weight of his famous surname, and has become an exacting professional. He specifies, "You have to protect your voice, and never force it. If I sing tomorrow and I'm not in perfect shape, I won't be able to sing for another month."

The former baker is in great demand around here. There's never a Sunday when he's not busy; if there are no weddings, there's always some gathering where he's the undeniable star. He has formed a group with three friends, and they sing together, have fun, and even make some money. "Six-hundred thousand lira in September," Fernando confides.

When Luciano was growing up, the Pavarottis lived in public housing on the outskirts of Modena, on via Giardini. Fernando and Adele confirm: "He was a very happy child, even if we were of modest means. But he never lacked anything." Luciano adds: "I never imagined that anyone could have any more."

In his autobiography Luciano wrote, "From our windows all you could see were fields and trees, a wonderful place for children to grow up. Sixteen other families lived in our building; all were either friends or relatives." The watchful guardians of this sunny, unclouded childhood were Fernando and Adele whose cheerfulness is complete and infectious. They are open, friendly people, and talk about Luciano's childhood without reserve.

As Signora Adele tells it, Luciano knew instinctively, at a very early age, what he would do with his life. Doubts only came upon him later, when he had to make a life-long choice. "He was three years old and he climbed up onto a stool pointing his finger upward, and saying, 'My daddy is a tenor, and I am a little tenor'."

"Signora Adele," I say, "Luciano once said 'I like to come across as charming'."

"It's true. His charm is a gift of nature, like his voice. His friends thought the world revolved around him, and adults liked him too. They competed for him at lunchtime, saying that he brought them good cheer and good humour. We were proud of our son, but wished that he would have been with us more often when we sat down to eat."

"How did Luciano do at school?"

"He took school with carefree cheerfulness, didn't work too hard, and had no problem passing. I would say that he never gave us any problems. Later on, in high school, he had a little trouble with Latin, but did well in maths."

"What was a typical day for little Luciano?"

"He never lay around in bed, but ran outside as soon as he could, and played soccer as long as possible. He dreamed of becoming a champion. He never ruled out the possibility of one day playing for Juventus, which is still his favourite team. Sometimes this passion of his caused us trouble. Every two weeks we had to buy him a new pair of shoes, or at least have his old shoes resoled. We weren't rich, and the shoemaker's bill weighed on the family budget. I remember that soccer was a passion that couldn't be controlled. Sometimes his teachers called us to school to tell us that Luciano wanted to interrupt class for a sudden game of soccer with his pals."

"But all and all, he was a well-behaved boy?"

"Well-behaved, I wouldn't really say. He often got into scuffles with his friends, but they were just squabbles, and didn't last long. Luciano never liked to be outdone, not even at sports."

I tell Adele, "Luciano said, 'Ever since I was little I had pluck, and lots of it'."

"He sure did. He always knew what he wanted. Sometimes he came home with a black eye, but he always said he'd blackened both of the other guy's eyes."

"Luciano knew he would be a tenor. When did outsiders start to realise this?"

"Very early, when he was about five. We had given him a toy guitar, and with it he sang some famous arias that he had learned by listening to my husband's records. At certain hours, however, his singing wasn't greatly appreciated. There were many times in the early afternoon when the neighbours would shut him up, yelling *Bastaa, Lucianein!* Enough Luciano!"

"Then would he come home with his head hung low?"

"Hardly. He brought his guitar home to go running after a

soccer ball. Toward the evening he would start singing again, excerpts from operas. One of his favourite arias was 'La donna è mobile'."

"A tenor for a son, a tenor for a husband! And you, Signora Adele, never infected by notes. Is it true that music moves you deeply? That you have never gone to one of your son's opening nights?"

"It's true. Music has moved me deeply ever since I was a little girl. It has always given me great emotions that make my heart burst. How could I follow first my husband and then my son? I used to go to the Teatro Comunale to hear the singers of the day, as soon as I could. Usually, though, I had to settle for the radio and the records that Fernando was always putting on the gramophone. For Luciano it was harder. Sometimes I got as far as the doors to the theatre, but then I had to run home. Only last year I finally decided to face one of Luciano's opening nights. I was anxious all day, as if it were my début. My heart was going a thousand miles an hour, then I calmed down and faced *L'Elisir d'amore*, The Elixir of love, at the Teatro Comunale of Bologna."

"Your husband never wanted to quit his job as a baker, even though many people told him he would have a good career as a singer. Is it true that this was out of fear?"

"Everything happened partly out of fear, but partly because anyone who works with bread loves it. Maybe it was a difficult choice; try asking Fernando."

Fernando confesses: "I had a genuine passion for my job, and I never had the courage to take risks. All those people, all those lights. I would have liked to sing, but I overcame my fear too late. It was 1980. We were in New York, and I was in the front row. Luciano finished an aria and then turned to the audience: 'Now you will hear my father'. Can you imagine!? He hadn't warned me, and the audience was applauding and smiling. I wanted to sink into the ground. Then I told myself, 'Fernando, the moment is ripe, now or never'. My legs turned to butter, I broke out in a cold sweat, but I managed to make it to the stage. Today I still wonder how I ever did it.

"When I was up there, my fear disappeared almost miraculously. The lights that had so terrified me were my salvation, because I couldn't see anyone. I could only hear that after the friendly applause there was a huge silence, and then I felt as if I were at home with my friends in one of the many churches of Modena, where I sing all the time. The orchestra started into César Franck's 'Panis Angelicus', and I went straight into it from beginning to end. There were six thousand people, but at the end, when the applause stopped, all I wanted to hear was Luciano's opinion. He hugged me and said, '*Bravo, Pavarotti*'. My face was all wet. I never asked him whether it was sweat or tears."

Signora Adele comments, "You should have realised it earlier."

I step in, "Signora, two tenors at home, wouldn't it have been a little too much?"

"Why? There are never enough beautiful voices. And my husband, let me guarantee you, would have been a great voice."

"Signor Fernando, once and for all tell us the truth, if you could do it all over again . . ."

"I would sing, I would try to overcome all my fears. But I would want to make sure that nothing changed for Luciano. I never thought a lot about myself, I always placed my family first, and deep inside I was always sure my son would become a great singer. When he was little I used to take him by the hand and bring him to sing in the choir of San Bartolomeo. The Lord loved us, and I think that sometimes something important comes of sacrifices. If that's how it was, I'm happy. I can't complain. I have had my satisfactions, too."

"It's true," Signora Adele confirms, "Fernando could have studied hard and become a great singer; he still has a respectable voice. We spend lovely days with our friends, and a few weeks ago we spent a wonderful afternoon together in Fanano. They wanted Fernando and his group for a concert in the parish church. Maestro Mosè Bursi was at the organ, the tenor Alberto Mattioli sang a splendid 'Ave Maria', and Fernando was applauded for his 'Caro mio bene', 'Pietà Signore', and 'Panis Angelicus'."

When Luciano comes home to Modena, he spends many hours with his parents, and the two Pavarottis compete in front of the harmonium. In her life, Signora Adele has had to worry not only about her son, but a couple of years ago about her husband as well. "A coldness and an unexplainable melancholy came over Fernando. He said he had lost his voice, and he seemed like a canary in a cage. He didn't want to leave the house. I was at his side all day long, saying, 'Try vocalising, you'll see that everything will go back to the way it was before'. My words made no difference. Luciano phoned from all over the world. 'Did Dad sing today?' Maestro Livio Borri, the director of the classical chorus, bombarded him with phone calls to shake him out of his apathy, and would bellow with that big voice of his, 'Shake yourself out of this lassitude!' It was like talking to the wall. I suffered, and even cried. Fernando sat in the armchair, barely moving. He wasn't even interested in his *bocce* friends, or in his *briscola* friends.

"One day I decided things had gone far enough. Without telling him, I invited over all the friends who had accompanied him in concerts, and asked them to sing. They sneaked in, one by one: Signora Gramostini, who is the organist for the group, Alberti, the violinist, Walter Cozzi, Ivo Maselli, Vaparelli, Bertoni and Dini. They surrounded his armchair and then, all of a sudden, intoned, 'Caro mio ben'. Fernando suddenly stood up, put his hand over his heart, just like tenors do, and came out with that voice from the good old days. I hid my face in my hands and shed a few tears."

"What did you tell Fernando?"

"*Te stè 'na carazza*, you were like a caress. Then I hugged him. We were as happy as two kids. Fernando wanted to keep singing, jumping from one corner of the room to the other. It seemed as if the sun had come back into our lives."

"Signora Adele, one more comment about Luciano."

"Luciano is the great joy of my life. When I think that God chose me to be his mother, I am overcome with emotion. It all seems like a dream or a fairy tale."

After his 'début' in New York, Fernando Pavarotti overcame his fear of the stage, and has sung in *La Bohème* several times, even in China. He is the most famous Parpignol in the world today. He has also set new goals for himself, and will probably sing in *I Pagliacci* in San Francisco, in the role of the peasant. His years in the chorus are far behind; next time his name will be on the billboard, close to his son's. Today the former baker is a happy, fulfilled man, with many memories. Gigli liked his voice, and so did Del Monaco, who picked him out of the chorus, asked him to step down, and said to him somewhat brutally, "Aren't you ashamed to be a baker? Your voice is better than mine." Pavarotti senior says, "I think he was joking."

At this point, Signora Adele suddenly shifts toward the harmonium and picks out the notes for '*Prendi l'anel ti dono*'. Fernando gets up from his chair, stands next to her, and sings with all the voice he has in his throat. His pharyngitis is gone, erased by an afternoon spent among memories. His wife gives him a big kiss and tells him once again. "*Te stè propria na carazza.*" She tells me, "I didn't want to tell him, but I've learned by ear. I only know how to use the white keys."

What people these Pavarottis are! What a wonderful life it would be if I could spend more afternoons like this. I stop at the door for a second and ask, "What does bread mean to you, Signor Fernando?" "It's love", he says. "Bread is people." He accompanies me to the courtyard, and as he goes down the steps he vocalises, "Aaaah, aaaeh, eeeah . . ."

A NEWSPAPER
CLIPPING

Where should I begin? With a début, obviously, but also with a newspaper clipping. Yes, a clipping is important in the life of a star. It is the palpable proof that you exist, that someone noticed you; it is the thing that in some way consecrated you. I think I was the person who wrote the first line about Pavarotti, out of friendship, because I immediately believed in his voice, but also because a unique character connected him to me: Bruno Storchi, the tenor's cousin, my friend, and a somewhat naïve sportswriter.

Bruno Storchi's house on via Amendola in Modena was my second home. Its doors were always open to me. Thinking about those years, I remember my return from my first job as a foreign correspondent in New York. Bruno decked the house and garden out with paper-chains, flowers, lights, and banners with things written in English.

He had many lives in the sense that in the morning he was a very disciplined bureaucrat in the Modena Sanitation Department, in the afternoon he was a director of bicycle races at the national level, and towards evening he became a reporter for the *Gazzetta di Modena* and dozens of other newspapers specialising in cycling. In his spare time, he dabbled in property and construction (he was a contractor), and came up with ideas for thousands of the most varied events. That, in short, is who Bruno Storchi was.

One morning he came to me at the *Gazzetta* and asked very simply, brusquely and almost resentfully, "When are you going to make up your mind to write something about Luciano?" When you are good friends with someone, sometimes you don't realise that they are becoming important. This is what happened to me with Pavarotti. But even in sceptical Modena someone had realised that Luciano would go far. Bruno Storchi actually told me, "You and I should get together and form a press office for him." Back in those days I dreamed of becoming a correspondent; I wanted a suitcase, not a desk. If I had only listened to him!

At any rate I wrote the piece. Until his dying day Bruno Storchi kept it in his wallet, folded and tattered, but valid proof that we had done something concrete for the man who would become the great Pavarotti. Luciano was very grateful to me for those lines. Our friendship was strengthened thanks to Bruno Storchi, whose two great passions were bicycling and Pavarotti. He followed all the races, whenever he could, and followed Pavarotti when he sang at any theatre in the region.

Bruno was also Luciano's first partner when the tenor began to think it might be a good idea to lose weight. Bruno himself was very thin, but his affection for Pavarotti was so great that he underwent the torturous fasting at the spa at Uscio, sharing the Spartan liquid diet and atrocious stomach pains that accompanied it, just so he could be close to Pavarotti. He kept watch over him inflexibly, but sometimes unavailingly, during these periods of abstinence.

Luciano's heart still has not healed from the wound left by his death. Storchi was almost bald, and some time ago, during a television interview, Pavarotti told me, "Whenever I see a bald man . . ." He was unable to continue, and did nothing to hide his tears from the cameras.

Very few people know that Luciano Pavarotti, out of

friendship for his jack-of-all-trades cousin, got involved in the most varied sports events, and was willing to follow the races of unknown amateurs because Storchi asked him to. Pavarotti would be the guest of honour, the chairperson of the jury, and the master of ceremonies, awarding trophies to the winners. Today it would no longer be possible, but back then he would do it for fun, for friendship, and for Storchi. For Bruno Storchi it was important that at the finishing line there be not only the winner, but also Luciano.

Storchi's life ended in a car accident. He was returning from an opening at the Arena of Verona, where he had gone to hear Pavarotti. Storchi was very near-sighted, and had eyeglasses with very thick lenses. Nevertheless, he always drove his Alfa-Romeo too fast. He failed to spot a streetlamp, and crashed into it. He was taken to the hospital, but insisted on being released immediately. I ran into him a few days later in Modena. His face was all bruised, one of his eyes was swollen, but as always, he was smiling and in a hurry. I asked him if he'd been to see a doctor to have some x-rays taken. He said that he saw no need for that, and didn't have the time. He took his leave saying, "I'm fine, see you soon."

We never saw each other again. A few days later he suffered from a brain embolism, and the 'bald man' disappeared from our lives. Today his widow's home still holds the memories and the nostalgia of those happy, carefree days, as well as the huge void left by a man who filled the lives of his friends and was the first press agent for Pavarotti.

Pavarotti told William Wright: "With each artist you see - good or bad - you never know what little bundle of encouragements they carry around with them to support their career, what little pats on the back from what hands, what newspaper clipping, what word of hope from what teacher. I suppose that the so-called faith in ourselves is the foundation of our talent, but I am sure these encouragements are the mortar that hold it together." Bruno Storchi was an important part of that mortar, and when Pavarotti was saying these words he was almost certainly thinking of his old friend.

After my first articles Pavarotti was finally given an official review. It appeared in the *Gazzetta di Reggio* on 30 April 1961, after his début in *La Bohème* at the Teatro Municipale. Their music critic wrote: "The tenor Luciano Pavarotti sang with commendable good taste and vivid musicality, in addition to displaying a vocal apparatus that was equally penetrating and flexible. He was perhaps better liked than his fellow artists." To re-read these somewhat ingenuous lines today, after the flood of reviews that have rained down on Pavarotti, brings a smile to my face. They are somewhere between a medical handbook, with its talk of 'vocal apparatus', and an exercise manual where the same apparatus is deemed 'flexible.' But the review borders on the pathetic when it praises Pavarotti for his 'commendable good taste'. He was 'perhaps' better liked than his fellow artists. The stingy and arrogant critic certainly did not realise that he was witnessing an historic moment. Yet that review made Luciano's eyes light up with joy, and his heart, he confesses, "was filled with gratitude".

Friendship and affection play a large part in Pavarotti's life. At first, he suffered from the rivalry and moodiness of fellow artists and conductors. The journalist Ennio Cavalli asked him: "To be introduced every evening as the 'best tenor of the century' must take nerves of steel. Do you have them?" The tenor replied: "No tenor is absolutely 'the best'. Partly because very few make it to the top. Technical and personal qualities are not invented; you really have to ride the tiger. But you have to live through these situations before you can judge them."

When Cavalli insisted, "Do you feel like number one in every sense?" Pavarotti specified, "What counts is that I have reached my position, whatever it may be, without pushing other people aside. Some colleagues absolutely want the audience to like them. I like the audience. Maybe that's where the difference lies. If people applaud me, fine. Otherwise it means that I deserve to be applauded less."

His words reveal the human dimension and the fundamental realism that together constitute the two most important aspects of Pavarotti's character. The trajectory of Pavarotti's success can be explained by the fact that he worked his way up without forgetting the affectionate ties he has maintained since the first years of his career.

For example, Pavarotti always remembers that the first time he sang in *La Bohème* it was after having led a bohemian existence himself for several weeks in a small hotel in Reggio Emilia. "None of us had a penny, but we believed in ourselves and in the future." Naturally he arrived at the dress rehearsal in a state of great tension, and with his "heart in his throat". Pavarotti recalls: "I was as tense as a violin string, and I tried to figure out what Francesco Molinari Pradella, the conductor, thought of me. I knew he was not an easy man. Incredibly, his baton stopped in mid-air during my aria in the first act, and the orchestra stopped. In a glacial silence I heard the conductor's voice: 'Young man, if you sing like that before the audience, you will be triumphant'."

Was a magical accord established between the young tenor and the famous maestro at that moment? "Hardly," said Pavarotti. "Molinari Pradella had one moment of generosity that he instantly regretted." In fact, on opening night Pavarotti eclipsed one of the greatest batons of all time. How else could the maestro react except by being resentful, and silently furious? "Everyone was happy for me, except him", Pavarotti recalls. That truly happy day was overcast by the shadow of envy, a word whose meaning Pavarotti did not know, but with which he would have to deal repeatedly.

In the early days, Pavarotti experienced another difficult moment in Lucca, where a tough confrontation awaited him. The soprano was Rosanna Carteri. She had been legendary once, and was still a beautiful woman, but her voice was no longer enthusiastically greeted by the audience and the critics. Time passes for everyone, but la Carteri seemed unwilling to accept the harsh truth. Pavarotti immediately realised that the show-down would take place over the two most famous arias, 'Che gelida manina' ('The Cold Little Hand') sung by Rodolfo, and 'Mi chiamano Mimì'. This time the little hand would truly be cold, and already in rehearsal la Carteri was proving as implausible as Rodolfo's lover. Her glances were like arrows, and Luciano was dismayed; he still maintained the adoration of women that came from growing up in an almost totally female world, and this was the first time he had to deal with a woman who disliked his presence.

This second experience of jealousy was worse than his first, even if Tito Schipa would say after the performance: "You have a beautiful voice; keep singing without worrying about people who are jealous of you." That evening, despite the cold little hand, the tenor electrified the audience, and Mimì had to grit her teeth and realise that she was in the presence of a great voice. Yet Pavarotti had tried not to do his best for fear of quarrelling with a singer who was, in those days, a living legend of opera. Luciano would later confess to Wright: "Even though I wasn't singing my best with this unpleasant soprano, the Rodolfos I sang in Lucca went well and were a good experience for me. After all, it was the first time I had been paid to sing an opera - 80,000 lira for two performances."

The trial of Lucca proved that Pavarotti had made the right choice. He had taken a gamble when he asked his family: "Let me try; support me until I'm thirty. If I don't succeed in becoming a true tenor, I'll find another profession." After his difficulties in Lucca he realised he had won the wager. Pavarotti had met the challenge while staying true to a wise peasant philosophy that would always be one of the guidelines of his life. "I loved the land, I love the land, and if one day I have to make a final choice I would find a valid reason for living in the fields."

When someone once pointed out to him that in Modena you tell someone to go dig the fields when you want to insult them, Pavarotti replied, "Why should a blow of the spade be less noble than a high C?"

Going through a photo album with the journalist Renzo Allegri, Pavarotti said: "I love looking at these pictures because they take me back in time. These photos document my true roots. What came later is a beautiful, a very beautiful thing, but it has not changed the substance of my personality and my true value. If I had not been so lucky with singing, if I had not become famous, I would still have been Luciano Pavarotti. I would still have had the affection of my parents, the respect of my friends, the love of my wife Adua, who married me convinced that I would become a good elementary school teacher. These are the things that matter, and I never want to forget them."

The volumes that contain the photographs from a great career have come to occupy an entire bookcase, but the first is the most important. Pavarotti explains, "This is the one that contains the most intimate pictures and memories of my childhood and early youth, when I was still poor and unknown. To be happy but poor is a wonderful condition." Going through the family album with Allegri, Pavarotti stopped at a picture taken in Modena's public gardens. He is with Adua, to whom he had recently become engaged. Pavarotti described that time as follows: "We were engaged for a long time, but spent so many happy days together! My family didn't have a car. My father went to work on a motor-bike. Every so often he would lend it to me for a few hours. I would pick Adua up and we would go for wonderful rides. During the summer my father gave me a special present: he lent me the motor-bike for a whole day, so by leaving early in the morning I could take Adua to the seaside. Our vacation consisted of that single day, but we felt like we had touched heaven. During the difficult years of working my way up, waiting to become established, Adua was of great help to me. She didn't love opera, but she encouraged and supported me. Time went by. My friends were all settled in their chosen professions and married. I was still penniless. I wanted to marry Adua, but how could I support her?"

THE "LUCIANO PAVAROTTI" CLUB IS BORN

I n 1979, the surveyor Gianni Carretti went to see the theatre
impresario Carlo Alberto Cappelli, and proposed that the
Carpi opera club be named after Luciano Pavarotti.
Cappelli said, "Forget about it." Pavarotti was well on the
road to his greatest triumphs, and was celebrated all over the
world. *Time* magazine had not yet featured him on its cover, but
it would do so two years later. This was to be his definitive con-
secration.

Carretti is the club's vice president. Commendatore Cappelli,
who had only recently accepted the position of honorary president, said at the time: "Pavarotti is great and will become even
greater, but I don't think we need to make him into a legend yet.
There will be time." But Carretti insisted. The previous year he
had witnessed the demise of the Bondeno Opera Club, and had
broken away from the club with a majority of the members. He
intended to do something new. Cappelli warned him: "Go ahead
and try, but Pavarotti will say no."

So one hot August afternoon, Gianni Carretti went on a
pilgrimage to Saliceta San Giuliano. With him was the other
vice-president, Umberto Tardini, a houseware and hardware

salesman. They arrived sweating and without much hope, and above all without the blessing of the *Commendatore*. On the threshold of the Pavarotti house, Carretti told Tardini, "He'll say no, but he can't refuse us a glass of water." The first obstacle to get past was Franco Casarini, also known as Panocia, the tenor's faithful bodyguard. Panocia is from Correggio, the two messengers from the Opera Club were from Carpi, and there is an ancient rivalry between the two cities. But Panocia has a big heart. "I can put in a good word, but Luciano is too modest. I'm afraid he will say no." Adua didn't have much time to listen to them. She was fixing a curtain, and commented, "As far as I'm concerned, go ahead, if he likes the idea."

The "he" in question arrived two minutes later, in a summer shirt and shorts. Carretti bowed down, "Maestro if you could hear us out." Pavarotti stopped him right there: *Maestro, chi? Me am ciam Luciano . . . Gni megh.*" ("Maestro who? My name is Luciano, come with me.") Carretti and Tardini, intimidated and silenced, followed him into the garden and didn't know how to proceed. Pavarotti sensed their distress. "What can I do for you?" he asked. Gianni Carretti was finally able to breathe, "A glass of water, Maestro." "Knock it off with this Maestro," Pavarotti warned them, half-serious and half-joking. The glasses of water arrived, Carretti caught his breath and screwed up his courage while Pavarotti sat in his Mercedes with his feet on the ground. In two sentences the two vice-presidents of the Carpi Opera Club explained their idea.

Pavarotti grew quiet, and a minute went by that seemed like an eternity to the two men from Carpi. Then the tenor broke out in a guffaw. "In another city, even New York, I would have said no because some might accuse me of megalomania, but to my friends from Carpi I say yes, that would be fine." Gianni Carretti, who is a calm man, remembered: "I am always in control of myself, but I started to sweat, and not because of the heat. I swear I was in a cold sweat. Pavarotti accepting. Pavarotti refusing to be addressed formally or as 'Maestro'. I started to stutter, and another 'Maes . . .' almost came out of my mouth, before I quickly swallowed it, but I didn't know where to begin thanking him."

Naturally they celebrated with some cold lambrusco. "We returned to Carpi to tell our friends the news, and wished we had an aeroplane to get there more quickly." In an instant the bitterness they had experienced several months earlier was gone. The first to know that the club would carry Pavarotti's name was Enea Tamassini, the pastor of San Francesco's, who at the moment of the split had offered Carretta and his friends a room in the rectory for their meetings, and had also agreed to chair the association ("But only for a short time, the minimum it will take to get things started.") That evening they celebrated in Carpi, and dreamed of inaugurating the club's activities in Pavarotti's presence.

Are dreams forbidden? No, but even dreams can only be taken in small doses. Two months later Gianni Carretti went back to Pavarotti to request his presence at the inaugural night, and showed him a list of singers for a special recital. The tenor read the list and commented, "Beautiful voices, beautiful voices, but on the opening night I will sing, alone." Carretti still remembers: "Do you realise what kind of a man Pavarotti is? For us it was already wonderful to have him in the audience applauding, and instead he offered us a complete recital."

On the evening of November 15, 1979, Carpi seemed buffeted by a wind of wild joy: the Teatro Comunale was packed, and Pavarotti sang twenty-three pieces for two and a half hours straight. It was a great beginning for the Luciano Pavarotti Opera Club, and the results were not long in coming. Carretti and his friends wanted to offer good concerts, but also to help those who had been less fortunate in life. The room in the rectory was suddenly too small, and don Tamassini had to step down because his parishioners needed his attention. Gianni Carretti became president: "As they say, *onori ed oneri*, honour and onus. The first task was finding decent headquarters, the second was furnishing it, and the third was to build an organisation worthy of the name Pavarotti."

The profits from Pavarotti's recital, in accordance with the charter of the organisation, were given to charity. After the initial euphoria, Carretti and company had to deal with organisational problems. "The first days we thought about whether or not it was a good idea to leave don Enea's rectory, and wondered whether we shouldn't ask him for an extension, but then we decided to look for another solution. We continued to meet in the parish, though there could never be more than three or four of us there. One of us would sit behind the desk, the other on top. But there was no lack of good humour, and Pavarotti continued to send us signs of friendship and affection."

They finally found a headquarters on via Menotti. Almost two years had gone by since the day Pavarotti had accepted Carretti's proposal. The club's activities went well, and its membership increased day after day. "Through trips to opening nights and recitals at the Teatro Comunale of Carpi we became better known. The days when we bought the office desk at a bankruptcy auction seemed far behind."

Today, Gianni Carretti sits behind that polished and refinished desk; in the next room are two or three members and club "bureaucrats": Michele Micheli and Mirko Fornaciari are retirees who are devoted to Pavarotti. "They come here every morning at ten, break at twelve-thirty, and come back at four o'clock, remaining until seven." The headquarters is full of mementos and plaques. The walls are covered with pictures of tenors, sopranos, baritones and conductors. There is a young Toscanini, von Karajan, Mirella Freni, Raina Kabaivanska, and naturally there he is, higher than the rest, on the centre wall, even higher than Verdi and Puccini, in an oil painting by Gozzi. I ask: "Isn't it a bit too much, Carretti?" The president of the Opera Club smiles. "Maybe, but it was a choice dictated by my heart." There is also a half-bust of Pavarotti as Nemorino, more ugly than primitive. They put it with the other mementos so as not to disappoint its creator. "He worked with such enthusiasm," sighs Carretti.

I tell the president, "Pavarotti refuses to be a legend, but for you he seems something more, almost a religion." Carretti says: "Let's slow down a second. Luciano is first of all a great singer and then an exceptional friend. Now from that to say that he's a religion is too much. Obviously we admire him, otherwise this club wouldn't carry his name, but in Carpi we keep our feet on the ground. Don't forget that this is where sweaters were born, and before that there were wood-chips, work that requires humility, patience, and dedication. Carpi became the world capital of knitting because the people didn't abandon themselves to dreams too easily, and because they always found the courage to start over again. What Pavarotti means to the people is something you can read in the letters we get from all of Italy and half the world. When newspapers talk about cheering soccer teams, I thought, "Pavarotti deserves this and more, but in Carpi we don't like excesses."

I spoke to Carretti about his friendship with Pavarotti: "How are your relations with Pavarotti?"

"Straightforward, sincere, even a little confrontational. Since I became his friend, I've allowed myself to make observations here and there. Once I told him that in his place, I wouldn't have made a certain record that combined opera arias and folk songs. He replied, *An l'ho ménga fat per te*, I didn't make it for you. I was asking for that, I deserved it. That record was a big success."

"Everyone talks about Luciano Pavarotti's voice. What would you add?"

"That Pavarotti has an 'intelligent voice,' that he knows how to move both on and off stage, that he is loved by his fans, loves people, is a friend to his fellow artists and is a very humble man."

When it can, the Opera Club follows Pavarotti on his travels, even to far away places. They went to applaud him when he essayed his Ernani at the Metropolitan Opera in New York, and accompanied him to San Francisco, London and Paris. Whenever Pavarotti's name appears on a billboard, the president meets with the planning committee and they chart a plan of action. Hundreds of envelopes are sent out, gathering support, organising charter flights and bus trips. Days of travel, of vacation, and of Pavarotti.

"We don't only go to see Pavarotti," Carretti specifies. "We are interested in everything having to do with opera, in the most important performances, and in the great recitals." They are enthusiastic travellers. If Pavarotti isn't a religion for the Carpigiani, opera certainly is. Today there are more than one thousand members. The organisation's success is due not only to the tenor's name, but to their commitment. They give two awards: one for the most prestigious names, the others for those who have distinguished themselves in a particularly good year.

Since 1980, this last award has been given to Pavarotti (he was the first to receive it, and how could it be otherwise), and then to Renato Bruson, Raina Kabaivanska, Mirella Freni, Carlo Bergonzi, Katia Ricciarelli, Ruggero Raimondi, Lucia Valentini Terrani, José Carreras and Maria Chiara. Each of them received a golden skein. It is almost too easy to explain its meaning in Carpi, but Carretti specifies: "Of course this is the capital of knitting, but in this age of sophisticated technologies, it is good to remember that here they began with knitting needles and balls of wool."

The other prize carries the name of Carlo Alberto Cappelli, and every year it is given to a person who merits the three adjectives engraved on the plaque: "To the man, the artist and the friend."

Some of the most famous names in opera have stepped across the stage of the Carpi theatre, people who normally travel only when given a check with many noughts in the figure. But they come to Carpi for free. "And do you know why?" Carretti explains. "Because they believe in our work, they love us, and are happy to help us do something for those who have been wounded by life." The president of the Opera Club tells me that every year with their profits from the concerts they donate advanced equipment to hospitals, funds to the Lyda Borelli rest home for artists, and wheel-chairs to the handicapped. Nine or ten concerts a year allow them to send help where the need is greatest. Everyone works voluntarily, and not one lira goes into the treasury of the Opera Club, which is financed exclusively through membership dues. Twenty-thousand lira per person is enough to pay for the rent, the electric bill, and the stamps for the hundreds of letters that are sent to the most varied destinations.

There are only two other clubs named after Luciano Pavarotti in the world, one in London, and the other in Vienna. They are directed by two energetic women, Ms Irene Jones and Frau Jolanda Kloder. Carretti and his collaborators keep close contact with them, and together they organise long trips and concerts, and keep an eye on the most important voices in order to bring them to the attention of critics, but especially to bring them before the Carpi footlights. This is very important, because being applauded by the Carpi audience constitutes a graduation ceremony of sorts.

I continue my interview with Carretti: "I've heard it said that you are the claque put together by Luciano Pavarotti."

A spark of indignation appears in Carretti's eyes: "Whoever said that is a liar. We will do anything for Pavarotti, but we'll never be his claque. For that matter, does Pavarotti even need one? This is slander, because there are singers, some with big names, who look for, expect, and pay a claque. It's just one way to feel safe, protected from eventual pitfalls.

"In the 1980s, the entertainment world has been overwhelmed; we get live TV broadcasts from all over the world, voices can be doctored in the most sophisticated ways, but you maintain that there are still claques.

"Of course. A well-prepared claquer can earn 150,000 lira a night. Not only will we never do anything of the kind, but we always pay for our tickets, each one of us, religiously."

"You must be Pavarotti's guests sometimes."

"We have never asked him for that. Our relationship must be honest and free. He has to allow me to criticise one of his records, if necessary."

"A memory that troubles you."

"It bothers me, but not too much. My friendship with Luciano has not been affected. And I don't think you have to drink everything that is poured."

"Sometimes it must be hard to get tickets for an opening night."

"In those cases Adua helps us. She always succeeds in getting seats for members of the Opera Club. And if every now and then it's harder than expected, Pavarotti comes in at the last minute and solves everything with his . . . magic wand."

"When you travel abroad Pavarotti drinks a toast with you after the performance, naturally."

"No. It only happened once, in New York. He came to the restaurant and stayed for half an hour. Then he went to bed. Pavarotti is very scrupulous, and a true professional. We respect his discipline, and admire him for it. It would be nice to have him with us because he's wonderful company. But we're happy to wait for him outside his dressing room. Luciano hugs us, and spends a few minutes with us. He always says, "Thank you, you make me feel at home." He never refuses to see us, and expects us to be understanding."

"What have you learned about Pavarotti the man in following him all over the world?"

"That he is very loved. Especially by his younger colleagues. He understands them and helps them. He has never forgotten how hard it was for him in the beginning. He also pays a lot of attention to older people. Sometimes in the competitions he organises or for which he is a member of the jury, a sixty-year old man might appear, still sure that he is going to have a break-through. These things happen, there are those who live on illusions. Pavarotti listens to him patiently, affectionately, and if by chance the aria is not sung in the very best fashion, he does everything possible not to destroy that illusion forever. He asks, 'Do you have anything else you'd like us to hear?' "

Ever since Carretti founded the Luciano Pavarotti Opera Club in Carpi, Modena has exploded with jealousy. "And do you know why?" Carretti asks, "because in 1975 when Luciano was already the great Pavarotti, his fellow citizens still considered him a singer in the chorus." Carretti put his finger on the sore spot in the relationship that exists, or rather that existed, between Pavarotti and his hometown. Nowadays the town totally adores him, but it used to judge him too critically. The people of Modena held back his final apotheosis until he had triumphed the world over, then gave a giant concert that filled Piazza Grande and all the streets in the downtown area. On that occasion, in the name of the whole city, Maestro Alfredo Guidi wrote in the *Resto del Carlino* what should have been written ten years earlier:

"Pavarotti is an authentic native son, who can see himself in his fellow citizens, and knows how to communicate with them in an almost absolute way, above and beyond the musical line. He does this both when he expresses the softest of melodies, in his winning way, and when he affronts with vehement passion certain dramatic twists fraught with a tumescence, which on close inspection is not unlike a temperament we see in Terra Emiliana, a region that by no accident was the cradle and witness of Verdi's creative fervour."

Carretti asks, "Don't you think they should have written these things ten years ago?"

We go out onto via Menotti with the president and his assistants, Tardini and Renzo Magnani, an industrial photographer. Underneath the number 10 is a brass plaque engraved with the words *Circolo lirico culturale Luciano Pavarotti.*" It is nice and shiny. "We polish it every morning, you know," say pensioners Michele Micheli and Mirko Fornaciari.

DOING YOUR ALL
FOR LUCIANO

Franco Casarini, also known affectionately as Panocia, lives in a small house on the outskirts of Correggio. But he's arranged to meet me at the Teatro Comunale. He is tall, robust, with a face like Rod Steiger, and red hair streaked with white. "You must see our city theatre," he says. "It's from the nineteenth-century, a real jewel." We enter the lobby of the Teatro Comunale, where this season's tickets are on sale. "Take a good look at the theatre, then we'll talk about Pavarotti: this is a necessary introduction, do you understand? To talk about Luciano you need to do a little spiritual vocalising."

Signor Casarini came by bicycle. "Pedalling is good for me," he says, "I have to lose weight, too, like Luciano. I should go on a diet." It's time to go home to via Raffaello Sanzio. I ask him if I can offer him a lift in my car. Casarini accepts, then glances at his brand new elegant black bicycle. "What if someone steals it? It cost me a fortune, I had to pay in instalments," he jokes. He looks as if he were leaving his beloved behind. "How about if I take you on my bicycle?" he asks.

We ride through the streets of Correggio. It's a hot, autumn afternoon. The air is heavy with humidity. Casarini is doing well, pedalling in nice round strokes, like a long-distance racing cyclist.

Who would Franco Casarini be, were he not known as 'Panocia'? Just another of the many artisans in the lower Reggio area. Instead the name Panocia is famous in the opera world: it's the name of Pavarotti's best friend, bodyguard and driver, the only driver to whom Pavarotti entrusts himself and his Maserati when he has to travel. Whenever he can - which is almost always - Panocia follows Pavarotti to the ends of the earth, because as Luciano says, "You can't get by without a friend, ever." Panocia is a best buddy, someone on whom Luciano can always rely. Whenever he gets homesick, he calls home first, and then Panocia. But on Sundays, he calls Panocia first, in order to get the football scores, even if he's in Australia. Panocia supports Torino, Luciano is a Juventus fan. Every now and then this leads to heated telephone conversations.

But where did Franco Casarini get a nickname like Panocia, and how did he and Pavarotti become friends? Did Panocia discover Pavarotti, or was it the other way around? And finally, why is their friendship so solid, trusting, and without misunderstandings or bad feelings? Franco Casarini says, "I wouldn't know. It happened by chance, because one night I went to hear Luciano before he became 'The Big', as *Time* magazine called him."

I ask, "What did your father do?"

"He was a miller," Panocia answers readily, "like my five brothers and I."

"Did it ever strike you, Mr Casarini?" I ask him.

"Did what ever strike me?"

"That Luciano's father was a baker, while yours was a miller. There's bread in the middle, do you see Mr Casarini, there's flour between the two of you. It's the first and fundamental fact of life."

Panocia looks at me as if he were in a trance, and his eyes become soft like those of a child. Now he really looks like Rod

Steiger. He stutters, then he jumps out of his chair and hugs me. "You've unveiled a mystery. I've thought about it, you know, I've thought about it many times. Who knew why Luciano and I are such good friends? You've explained it. From now on, let's not be so formal with one other, is that all right with you?"

"Fine. But tell me Panocia, how was your passion for opera born?"

"I would say my story parallels Luciano's. A big family, grandparents, aunts and uncles, everyone working in the mill, in utter misery, and as a consolation in the evening, a gramophone and a few opera records. My father Gustavo played them over and over, and we sat in a circle listening. I was in ecstasy; I felt like I was in another world. My brothers, though, couldn't stand it. Finally they emancipated themselves, making a collective declaration: 'We can't take it any more. We would rather play *briscola* in the stable.' Since then they've been allergic to opera, and don't want to hear anything about it."

"You once sang a little."

"Yes, I made a few tries with Arrigo Pola, Pavarotti's teacher. But if the voice isn't there, it's useless to insist and fool yourself. I made a few appearances in the chorus, in my parish church of course, and by listening to records I became quite a connoisseur. I can tell if someone is a real singer right away, after the first measure. I am a big fan of voices, especially male voices."

"So opera is your first and greatest love."

"Certainly, my great love. When I was fourteen I cycled from Correggio to Verona with a group of friends to go to the Arena. The night Del Monaco sang in *Andrea Chenier* I told my friends, 'Let's go for a bike ride, hear Del Monaco, and then come back.' We got back at dawn, exhausted. My friends never set foot in a theatre again."

"And what happened with Pavarotti?"

"In 1960, the year he came in second at the Achille Peri international competition (which he would win in 1961), Luciano was one of the soloists in a concert at Bagnolo di Correggio. He sang a beautiful '*Quando le sere al placido*', and made a great impression on me. I told my father, 'This guy has great facility with his high notes.' "

"So you immediately predicted he would have a great career."

"I predicted nothing. I applauded him with great conviction."

"When did you realise that Pavarotti would become Pavarotti?"

"My father realised it before I did. The next year we went to Reggio Emilia, where he had his début in *La Bohème* after having won the Achille Peri competition, and my father said, 'He will become a great tenor'. 'Better than Del Monaco, Gigli, Di Stefano and Corelli?' I asked him. 'Better than all of them, the best ever', my father pronounced firmly."

Even when Pavarotti was just starting out, Panocia, who is almost the same age, was an authority on the opera world in Emilia, and he still is. When someone first appears before the footlights, they've almost always been sent to Panocia beforehand. 'Let's hear what Panocia says, it would be a good idea to hear Panocia's opinion.'

"So you matter more than the critics Celletti and Pasi?"

"Let's not exaggerate. Let's say that I have intuition, a nose. When I met Luciano Pavarotti I was a consultant for the theatre association of Emilia Romagna, ATER, and the vice-president of some opera clubs."

"And you're funny, a music fanatic who knows his stuff without the pretensions of certain critics."

"If people say I'm funny, I like it. If they say I make no mistakes in my judgements, I hope it's true. With Pavarotti I was right. The night Luciano sang *Rigoletto* in Reggio Emilia, I went to his dressing room and asked, '*Vint a cà mia a zèina?*, Would you like to come to my place for dinner?' When he did his first *Elisir* in this area, I renewed the invitation, and Pavarotti accepted. He came with Adua and Fernando. A big meal of *maccheroni al pettine* with rivers of lambrusco. That's how our friendship began. Exactly twenty-two years ago."

"Let's take a step back, Franco Casarini, a.k.a. Panocia: where did you get your nickname?"

"Because when I was little I was red and round like an ear of corn (pannocchia)."

We go outside for a while, leaving the photo album on the table, and abandoning the Pavarotti books and records. Casarini accompanies me to the gate. On a pillar is a ceramic tile with a hand-painted ear of corn. "It is our family coat-of-arms. Some people inherit one, others have to invent one. Is mine worth less than anyone else's?" He laughs.

"Who makes up the Panocia family?"

"My wife Silvana and my children Adriana and Gustavo. Gustavo is a draughtsman, and the rest of us are in business together."

"The Pavarotti-Casarini company, I suppose."

"Not by a long shot! Pavarotti and I are friends, and naturally Adua and my wife are friends, and my daughter is friends with Luciano's daughters. But we do not do any business deals in opera, as Luciano's American friends say. We have a small embroidery company. With a couple of supermodern machines we reproduce well-known designs, signatures, and labels on sweaters."

"Getting back to Pavarotti, and your untarnished friendship, you must have had some difficult moments?"

"And how! Once when Luciano came back from the United States, I went to Malpensa airport as usual to drive him back to Modena. At a certain point they started saying the aeroplane was late. There was a fog so thick you could cut it with a knife. Those of us from lower Emilia are used to the fog, but that day it had a strange effect on me. I kept telling myself, 'Calm down, Panocia'. There wasn't much to be calm about. All at once the TWA workers closed their windows and stopped giving us information. We were there waiting, minute after minute. I felt like I was dying inside. At one moment someone from the company came and opened his arms: 'The airplane has crashed'. I don't know who that man was, nor who had sent him. But he must have been an imbecile, because a few seconds later another man arrived and said: 'The news is not true. The airplane has not crashed, it's in the air over Milan, but has to make a difficult, almost impossible landing'. You can imagine how I felt in that moment, and how the other people waiting felt. Some were waiting for their fathers, their husbands, their wives, their children.

"Finally the plane reached the airport and began its descent. We could make out its shape, but then it disappeared into the fog. A few seconds later there was a crash. Ambulances were wailing and firetrucks were roaring. The plane had landed in the worst way, and was literally split in two. Some people were wounded. Luciano finally slid off the plane after helping a woman from Detroit to get off who had frozen with fear in her seat."

When Pavarotti arrived in the Malpensa terminal, Panocia was waiting for him with open arms. "I'm not going to come to meet you any more," he stuttered, not knowing whether to laugh or cry. Pavarotti put a hand on his shoulder. They went to the car, and drove back to Modena. Panocia said, "If you really need me, I'll be there the next time too."

"Of course," Pavarotti answered.

"A nice memory, Panocia," I said.

"I have many nice memories. But one is better than all the others. In August 1988 we went to Göteborg in Sweden for a recital by Luciano. On the podium was Maestro Leone Magiera, who led the Stockholm Philharmonic Orchestra. The day of the dress rehearsal Luciano came up close to me and whispered 'Now or never'. 'What?' I asked him. 'This is your chance to sing in a great theatre'. 'You're crazy!' I replied. Laughing, Luciano pushed me toward the stage and winked at Magiera. The conductor started up with 'Mamma'. I don't know how, but there I was in front of a microphone singing with all my heart in front of five or six hundred people. You know, it wasn't that bad!"

"In that moment you thought that maybe you'd made a mistake not to attempt an operatic career."

"No way. It was a joke that was pulled off well. I know how to stay in my place."

"Your trips must be full of jokes."

"Yes, Luciano is cheerful until a few minutes before the

curtain goes up. Then a subtle tension comes over him, he goes looking for a nail, and he won't speak with anyone. I think the funniest story has to do with a recording of _Rigoletto_ that Luciano made in Vienna in 1982. I went with my daughter Adriana and his daughter Cristina. In Vienna Pavarotti stays at the Imperial. He always stays at the same hotels, and there is always a room ready for him - the same room, if possible. But that day four of us checked in, and the hotel manager regretfully told us, 'We can only find you two rooms at the most'. 'We'll manage,' Luciano offered '_Mè e te a durmàm insàm_, you and I will sleep together'." Cristina and Adriana shared the other room. It was the first time Pavarotti and Panocia had slept in the same room. They turned out the lights, and said good night to each other. But it would be anything but a good night. A few minutes after falling asleep, they woke up and realised that both snored with tenorial vigour.

"Now what can we do?" Luciano asked. "I'll sleep in the hall on a mattress," Panocia proposed. "Don't even think about it," Pavarotti answered. "All we can do is take turns, like sentinels: one hour you sleep, one hour I sleep." So that's what they did. In the morning they took turns using the shower, first Luciano and then Panocia.

"Who knows why," continues Panocia, "but as we were getting dressed we started badmouthing our wives, saying the usual things about them. I was punished for it: bending down to tie my shoes, I was paralysed into a right angle. They had to carry me into the car, and that time Pavarotti drove me all the way to Modena. In order not to scream in pain, I had to stay bent over in the Maserati, which is wide but low. I had to hug the seat with my head down, so my rear end was where my head would normally have been. We travelled this way for hundreds of miles. I still wonder what the people we passed on the road must have thought when they saw the great tenor's face, and next to it a backside that, as you can see, is quite voluminous."

Two weeks later Panocia was operated on for a herniated disc at the Modena hospital.

"Who is the victim, you or Pavarotti?"

"I would say Luciano. In Felino, a town in Emilia Romagna famous for its pork sausages, salami and ham, we came across thirty-three *coppas* (cured necks of pork) that seemed wonderful. I bought ten and Luciano took the rest. We put them in storage, and when we wanted them, I would get one for me, one for him. Whether it's because I'm a connoisseur, or because I'm lucky, I always got the good ones. All three *coppas* that I took out for him had some defect."

"It's hard to take you seriously."

"You try it, ask him. The same thing happened with two bottles of *grappa*: very fine and rare. When we got back to Modena, one of them was broken. 'It's yours', I told him. Luciano took the blow. 'OK', he sighed."

"But he gets back at you sometimes."

"Every time we play *briscola*. *L'è un gran lèder*, he's a big cheat, and refuses to lose. He wants to win at all costs, and if he hadn't become a great singer, he would have been quite a hustler. He switches the card with surprising ability, like an old pro."

"Do you ever criticise each other?"

"I accuse him of not having sung *Otello* yet. I torture him psychologically. It's his opera. He's going to have to make up his mind to do it."

"And he?"

"He wishes I had opened a restaurant in New York, because he says my wife is a great cook. Maybe he's right, but I'm fine here, this is where my friends, my roots are, and I can see Pavarotti every time he comes back to Italy and when I go on tours with him."

"What is Pavarotti to you?"

"A brother."

"And then?"

"A great voice, with a great mind."

Panocia accompanies me to the porch. There's a long table where great singers and famous athletes have dined.

"Franco Casarini," I suggest, "maybe you would have been Panocia even without Pavarotti."

94

He objects. "I would have been half a man. I started to culti-
vate his friendship early, and you can't imagine how opera helps
bring people closer."

"What does Pavarotti do when he comes to your house?"

"He goes straight to the refrigerator."

"So good-bye diet!"

"He has a little trouble, but he resists, and closes it. Since he
has gotten back in shape, we're trying to keep him from 'suffering', we adapt to his eating habits, making do with a steak. Sometimes he sighs, 'But your wife's _maccheroni al pettine_, but your
lambrusco...' Here and there we cheat a little, but not too much."

"Why is Luciano Pavarotti your best friend?"

"Because he can be quiet if he doesn't want to talk, and sleep
in the car if he wants to. And because I don't smoke. Is that too
little?"

"Driving Pavarotti in your car must be some responsibility."

"I floor it, because he's always in a hurry. And he trusts me
absolutely."

"You were on television with him, on _Domenica in._"

"We got some good laughs out of that one, too. There were
many famous TV stars. Before we went in, he took me by the arm
and whispered, '_A m'arcmand, degh bèin ch' a soun un to amigh_',
make sure you tell them I'm a friend of yours."

On a cupboard is a big picture of a Santa Claus with a
prominent nose and big brown cat eyes under a silly cap. It's hard
to recognise Franco Casarini. In this disguise, he loses all
resemblance to Rod Steiger.

"Every year," Panocia explains, "I dress up this way on
Christmas Eve to entertain my family and some friends."

I ask for a technical judgement from Franco Casarini.

"Our friendship aside, Pavarotti really is the greatest tenor of
the last fifty years because of the size of his repertoire. Like the
famous cyclist Coppi: good at uphill, speed and long-distance. In
some operas he's the best ever. When we go into a theatre
together, he jokes, 'You enter as an owner; I enter as a working
man'."

PAVAROTTI IN THE
MOVIES

In the autumn of 1981 the film producer Peter Fetterman
came to Italy. He had an appointment with Luciano Pavarotti to convince him to shoot a film with the prestigious
Metro Goldwyn Mayer studio. Those were the years when
the jealous Modenese were wondering if the Americans had
taken full possession of Pavarotti's heart and voice. In the United
States, where theatres and multinational companies were
competing for him all the time, the name Pavarotti was everywhere. Christening a product with his name was a guarantee of
success. A film with Pavarotti as the protagonist could only be a
success, a great business deal.

Luciano was amused by the idea, and agreed to it immediately.
For years Fetterman had thought of casting him as the star of a film
biography of Enrico Caruso, but on this they disagreed. "Too big
for me," Pavarotti modestly claimed, "there's no sense in making
comparisons." Now Peter Fetterman was back in the fray after
finding a story by the English writer Anne Piper in which an Italian
tenor suddenly loses his voice during a tour of the United States. He
falls in love with the female doctor who helps him to recover rapidly
and return to the stage. The film was called *Yes Giorgio*.

Pavarotti took the producer to Giorgio Fini's restaurant to discuss the project, and among the details they discussed was the leading man's name. The dinner was very elegant, and Fini outdid himself in the varieties of dessert. To show his appreciation Fetterman said, "Why not give your name to the tenor?"

Giorgio Fini accepted, and realised that in addition to being fun, it would be good publicity for his products. In that moment his namesake came to life. But instead of golden tortellini, the namesake offered notes.

Giorgio Corzolani, a journalist, wrote an entertaining essay on the relationship between Pavarotti and the cinema. His analysis of the film leads one to believe that its outcome was not quite as exciting as Fetterman had hoped.

"Should we deduce that in this case Pavarotti made a bad move?" I asked Corzolani.

"That seems excessive," he replies. "It was certainly no triumph, but in terms of box office, it was not even disappointing. In Italy the film was greeted with hostility and indifference. The critics panned it, but luckily the image of Pavarotti the tenor came out of it undamaged."

"How did the film do in the United States?"

"In the United States Pavarotti is an indisputable idol. People who were never able to hear him in the theatre were happy to become acquainted with his voice, and grateful to the film's producer."

"But why such a shower of criticism?"

"Critics were bothered by the script and by the story, which was considered old-fashioned, and irrelevant to a 1980's audience." Corzolani continues, "But let's look at the plot in outline. The film is a love story with long musical parentheses that begins in Italy and continues and ends in the United States. The opening scene is in Capodimonte, a small town on the shores of Lake Bolsena. Giorgio Fini has returned to Italy interrupting an American tour to sing at a friend's wedding, but a jet quickly carries him back to his second homeland. Here the tenor has one success after the other in operas, concerts and recitals. His triumphant career has only one blemish: the Metropolitan Opera in New York. Giorgio Fini cannot forgive the Met for an unfortunate evening when he was booed by the audience because of a series of technical difficulties. Since then Giorgio has refused to set foot there. When he returns to Italy, the invitation to sing at the most prestigious theatre in New York is renewed.

"This makes the Italian tenor so nervous that he loses his voice. While Giorgio is rehearsing 'La donna è mobile' for a Boston concert the notes stick in his throat. To his panic and that of his impresario (the actor Eddie Albert), the doctor who is sent to treat him is female. 'I've lost my voice, but I'm not going to let a woman treat me,' Giorgio Fini grumbles with an exaggerated Italian machismo. The doctor doesn't lose her cool, and senses that the tenor's problem is psychological, and not vocal. She convinces him that he is suffering from Steimenz' syndrome, a nonexistent illness, and gives him a booster shot. The shout Giorgio gives when she sticks the needle in proves that his voice has miraculously returned. Dr Pamela Taylor (played by Kathryn Harrold) doesn't just impress the tenor with her medical skills: Giorgio Fini stubbornly and relentlessly tries to date her, and she cannot resist him for long. The affair begins, but the singer makes the young doctor swear that she will not fall in love with him (he has a wife and children in Italy).

"Amid dinners, receptions, concerts, romantic weekends and flights in a Montgolfier balloon, the love story unfurls against a beautiful backdrop filmed in Los Angeles, Boston and San Francisco. But a shadow is always lurking: despite his triumphs, Giorgio Fini cannot muster up the force to return to the Met. Pamela is the one who convinces him, by throwing a pie in his face.

"Giorgio is so happy and moved by his new début in New York that he cannot resist the temptation to call and tell his wife Carla in Italy. He hopes that Pamela won't hear, but she hears everything. Convinced she can no longer go on pretending, she declares her love to Giorgio. Right then and there Giorgio decides to leave, and asks Pamela only to let them spend their last moments together in America peacefully, without worrying about his life in Italy. After sitting in the front row at the Italian tenor's triumphant return to the American temple of opera as Calaf in *Turandot*, the doctor decides to leave him. A part-time love is not enough for her."

"Corzolani, from your summary the film doesn't sound like a big deal. To me it sounds pretty banal."

"The love story between Pamela and Giorgio was very Hollywood. It's not that the producer and director wanted to make a low budget, second-rate film. The film's one hundred and thirteen minutes and cost 21 billion lira. In addition to the location shots, the film was shot at MGM's Culver City studios. One of Giorgio Fini's concerts was performed live at the Hatch Shell in Boston.

"The director was no minor figure: Franklin J. Schaffner had directed *Papillon*, *Patton* (which earned an Oscar for George C. Scott), *The War Lord*, *Nicholas and Alexandra*, *The Best Man*, *The Boys From Brazil* and *Planet Of The Apes*. Kathryn Harrold, in the role of Pamela, has acted in *Pursuit*, *Modern Romance* and *The Hunter*.

"Despite all this, the film didn't go over well. Why did Pavarotti get involved in this venture? Didn't he think he was taking a big risk? Lucky for him fortune did not abandon him even on this occasion. When *Espresso* talked about the willingness of Luciano and his colleagues to try varied experiences, it came out with a ferocious title, '*I tenoracci*', those awful tenors.

"Pavarotti is well-loved throughout the world, and this roadside accident, if you wish to consider it an accident, has already been forgotten. If you think about it, there's a very simple explanation: Pavarotti wanted to have a good time, and he did. This proves his enthusiasm, his youthful desire to try new artistic paths, his almost incredible adaptability to the most diverse situations and circumstances. These are the characteristics that make him such a special star in the opera world."

"But Corzolani, what part does music have in this decidedly Hollywood film?"

"It's fundamental, I would say. There are opera excerpts as well as traditional and modern songs. Two conductors played themselves: Emerson Buckley and Kurt Herbert Adler. Pavarotti sings many opera arias: 'Donna non vidi mai' from Puccini's *Manon Lescaut*; 'Ciel e mar' from Ponchielli's *Gioconda*; 'Una furtiva lagrima' from Donizetti's *Elisir d'Amore*; 'La donna è mobile' from Verdi's *Rigoletto*; and 'Nessun dorma' from Puccini's *Turandot*, the opera chosen for Giorgio Fini's triumphant return to the Metropolitan."

"There was also Schubert's 'Ave Maria', Leoncavallo's 'Mattinata', 'Santa Lucia', 'Oh Sole Mio' and two American songs, 'I Left My Heart In San Francisco' and the beautiful 'If We Were In Love', which received an Academy Award nomination for best song. I think that the quality of the film aside, the price of the ticket was a bargain for anyone who loves good music."

"No one would argue against that, but it could have been a better film, to avoid the heavy critical drubbing."

"There's always room for improvement, certainly. *Yes, Giorgio* did not obtain the success that the producer expected. Maybe the public prefers Pavarotti on stage. A film of this type might have seemed almost blasphemous."

"The critics were very harsh."

"*Yes, Giorgio* was criticised for being too sentimental and unrealistic. The star was told that he shouldn't have participated in it."

"But what did Pavarotti have to say about the experience?"

"In many interviews Luciano said 'The movie has something that I like, but that is considered a flaw today: it's a clean love story, with a traditional development and ending; something that could have happened to anyone'."

"But although the ending is full of so-called good feelings, and the protagonist ultimately returns to his wife, the Catholic Committee of the United States placed *Yes, Giorgio* on its list of prohibited films."

"That seems a bit extreme. Americans often exaggerate, and I think that our Luciano was somewhat offended by that decision."

"Why were they so tough?"

"The censors considered the film offensive to public morals because it represented an adulterous story on the screen."

Corzolani thinks that *Yes, Giorgio* should be read historically, in terms of the relationship between opera and film.

"The film world has not relied on the figure of a popular tenor to fill up cinemas since the times of Beniamino Gigli," he claims. "It's not that there was any shortage of singers on the set; what I mean to say is that Luciano Pavarotti's film is special because it was constructed entirely around the star. This is exactly what used to happen in the past for the great opera stars, from Caruso to Lily Pons, Gino Bechi and Tito Schipa. It recreated a film genre that died out in the early 1950s with Gigli."

"But times have changed, and you can hardly call those films great films to begin with."

"They weren't very good movies. Only Pavarotti, because of his huge popularity, was able to rediscover and retrace a path left behind decades ago by the great stars of opera. This justifies the linearity and simplicity of the plot. Even for the divas of the past, the screenplay often consisted of a naïve story that gave the star frequent opportunities to show off his or her singing. *Yes, Giorgio* is important historically as the last chapter in a fascinating novel of connections between movies and opera stars."

"It's been said that Pavarotti handed himself over to Hollywood with his hands and feet tied."

"I think *Yes, Giorgio* as the ideal meeting of the country of the Oscars and a tenor who has never hidden his propensity for experimenting with new approaches, with being a pioneer in the use of every tool for the dissemination of an image that modern technology has to offer."

"Some people criticised Pavarotti for being too careless in his career decisions."

"Pavarotti is always extremely disciplined in his work. With this film, I repeat, he just wanted to have fun. Of course there has been plenty of criticism of the eclecticism that has led him to express his art in the most varied places and ways over the past twenty-five years. Not everyone liked Pavarotti singing 'Mamma' and 'Non ti scordar di me.' Some purists have even objected to his concert with Frank Sinatra and his mega-recital in New York's Central Park."

"Some say that only the most rigorous choices will allow an opera singer to achieve the highest artistic goals."

"Luciano Pavarotti is always improving, and with this I don't come close to describing him," Corzolani maintains.

"He has proved again and again that he is a perfectionist, which makes it possible for him to capture the spirit of every character he brings to the stage, to render each of his nuances vocally. Above all he represents a phenomenon that eludes any classification or comparison with any singer of the recent past."

"Will Pavarotti try again?"

"If he feels like having fun, the possibility is there. For that matter, *Yes, Giorgio* was not his only foray into cinema. He also made a film of the opera *Rigoletto* with the French director Jean-Pierre Ponnelle, done with all the realism that a modern production can get from a camera. This *Rigoletto*, thanks in part to Pavarotti, is one of the best and most successful examples of the recent renaissance of opera films. Forty years ago the French scholar Henry Colpi made an intelligent observation: 'Opera films will have potential only when directors dedicate to them the same fervour and talent that Laurence Olivier dedicated to Shakespeare. For now, opera films can only publicise productions and voices reserved for the world capitals and La Scala.' "

"In conclusion . . ."

"In conclusion I would say that if Pavarotti committed a venial sin with *Yes, Giorgio*, in *Rigoletto* he was extremely convincing both as a singer and actor. I hope that Rigoletto will not remain an isolated chapter of his career, but that with the help of talented directors like Ponnelle, he will give new vitality to opera films, a genre in which the public is increasingly interested."

"Is Luciano Pavarotti a good actor?"

"In *Rigoletto* he was not only in splendid vocal form, but he conveyed emotions like a true actor."

PAVAROTTI'S PHOTO ALBUM

The first photo of Pavarotti was taken in 1937. He is holding a big ball: a globe of the world covered with stars. Signora Adele asked the photographer to liven up the image with a few touches of colour, and the cheeks of the young Pavarotti are tinged with a soft pink that brings out his eyes, which would remain the same year after year, even forty years later. They are sharp, smiling and childlike, with the unwavering gaze that millions of fans have come to know.

I leaf through Pavarotti's private and public album with Professor Corrado Fanti of the University of Bologna, who studies images. Together we try to understand something more about this character from this unique evidence.

According to Professor Fanti, the pictures taken before Pavarotti went on the stage reveal a contemplative attitude, as if he did not want to be led astray by distractions: "You can already see a precise life plan in Pavarotti as a boy." In those years Pavarotti dreamed of becoming a football champion, and would debate over whether to be a teacher or insurance agent, convinced all the while that it was his destiny to rise above mediocrity.

In 1965, after his great adventure had already begun, the tenor is getting off an aeroplane in Miami to sing in *Lucia di Lammermoor* opposite Joan Sutherland. Fanti notes that the photographer caught him by surprise, capturing a certain determination and gutsy attitude. One day Sutherland would say: "Luciano has always known how far he could push his public, what he could get from them, and I think he enjoys managing himself. He is very career-oriented; he loves singing, loves the response he gets from the audience, loves the high pay he receives. He loves everything. Why shouldn't he?"

Yes, why shouldn't he? In fact, the first time the people of Modena honoured him with the Carlotta Prize in 1965, Pavarotti offered himself to the photographer's lens with absolute spontaneity. Fanti says: "This picture brings out the intense satisfaction of someone who has achieved a goal that is important, even if it is intermediary, and that follows long preparation. Pavarotti is aware his picture is being taken, but his pose doesn't conceal the spontaneity of this serene feeling. His expression is joyful, but it nonetheless conveys great determination and the wish to continue."

In December 1965 Pavarotti was photographed in front of La Scala. Corrado Fanti points out: "He has a newspaper in his hands, and reading a newspaper is one way to have an image that looks spontaneous, even if it is posed. The theatre is his backdrop, and despite the newspaper he holds, Pavarotti is thinking about how to present himself, how to make his mark. This picture shows a serious face and a cautious smile, but it also reveals an impetuous expression of great character, and a determination to fill the surrounding space with his personality."

I suggest to Fanti: "Let's take three phases in Pavarotti's life: a dinner with friends in 1968, another convivial meeting with the members of Modena's Rossini Chorus, and a solo shot holding a picture of Caruso. How can we read these images?"

"The most relevant characteristic," Fanti points out, "is an expression that though ironic, is shaded with melancholy, arising from a profound humanity. However, I think it might be worthwhile to take a closer look at a picture taken by surprise in 1973 in Vienna, where Pavarotti was recording *La Bohème.*

"Pavarotti was photographed during a moment of intense concentration, bringing a pencil to his lips, looking down, into the distance, almost into infinity, and lost in his thoughts. Von Karajan and Mirella Freni appear in the same picture. The conductor appears to be concentrating, too, but is also mindful of what is going on around him. Pavarotti seems to be completely absent from the dialogue, withdrawn and far away from the others because he is deeply caught up in his own thoughts. But a careful reading shows that he is actually extremely close to his colleagues and to the conductor: his concentration leads him to the focal point of the problem."

"What about Pavarotti on stage?"

"On stage Pavarotti's gestures and poses are theatrical. Their theatricality, however, is not just pretending, not just acting, but an underlying professionalism that involves his entire being and psychology, but without violating them. Pavarotti's theatricality is a spontaneous pretending, an authentic theatricality inasmuch as it seems to correspond fully to himself. Performing never alienates Pavarotti from himself - on the contrary. It brings out the complete form of his personality on stage, which allows him to express himself very intensely."

"In Pavarotti's album, he sometimes appears in make-up before, during and after a performance. What is under the greasepaint?"

"Pavarotti's face, sometimes still heavily made up, can reveal a kind of tiredness underneath his contented, vigorous smile; this isn't a sign of withdrawal and sad thoughts, but a satisfied tiredness that follows the hard work of singing."

"But what identity emerges from Pavarotti's photo albums? How can you go beyond the stereotype?"

Fanti says: "I think Pavarotti is strong and aggressive, but some private pictures show us a serene, discreet, genuinely intimate man. The photos also reveal his willingness to laugh and his friendliness backstage after the curtain has fallen. Pavarotti's official seriousness is never overdone; if anything he's very composed. By the same token his professionalism never seems artificial to me, but rather like the natural result of commitment and high professionalism."

"In pictures taken on stage many actors look as if they were busy pretending they were doing something or other with a specific expression; they stare into space, and you can tell there's no reality in front of them, only painted scenery and make-believe situations."

"But the expression in Pavarotti's eyes is that of someone who observes and sees, even if the only thing before his eyes is the huge dark space out of which the public is looking at him. Pavarotti's eyes know how to look at the audience, but they also see the real situation he is translating into music. His eyes are not absent, even if there is no absence of make-believe. What he really sees is concealed by the absolute presence of something that his eyes see beyond the real, a deeper reality."

I point out that, "When Pavarotti bows to the audience, he does so in a simple, friendly way. In that moment he is anything but a *divo*."

Fanti comments, "In effect, his bow is not a perfunctory act, but something deeply felt, warm, human, charming, a way of expressing friendship and gratitude. He doesn't put on the airs of a star, but shares instead in the joyous happiness of an event he has lived together with the audience, with whom he has created an active, careful harmony."

"Let's take a look at Pavarotti with some American presidents: Carter, Reagan. He looks very friendly."

"I'm not afraid of engaging in regional rhetoric," Fanti declares. "Pavarotti always shows his Emilian character, the features of a culture that you can even hear in his notes, a way of presenting himself as tied to a land, a tradition. Pavarotti always expresses the simple joy of a man profoundly aware of his art. He knows that he is the bearer of this art, its interpreter and its instrument, almost, so he has no egocentric vanity or awareness of his special merits. He has the humility of one who realises that

*Luciano Pavarotti, aged 3, with his father
Fernando and mother Adele.*

A Luciano ascoltami e
arriverai certamente !!
studia e si tenace / sincerai
1957 Arrigo Pola

Opposite page:
Pavarotti in
I Puritani *in the*
Seventies.

This page, left:
Fernando and Adele
Pavarotti.

Below: *Luciano*
with his friend,
bodyguard and
chauffeur Franco
Casarini.

Right: *Luciano at the Carpi club that bears his name. From the left: maestro Leone Magiera, Carlo Maria Badini (Superintendent of La Scala), Gigi Reverberi (Director of the Teatro Comunale of Reggio Emilia), Pavarotti and Gianni Carretti (President of the Carpi Opera Club).*

Below: *Franco Chiusoli (President of the Confederation of Co-operatives in Emilia-Romagna) presents Pavarotti with a saddle; on the right is Angelo Nicoletti (Chairman of Bologna Airport).*

Above: *Pavarotti
with singer-
songwriter
Francesco Guccini.*

Left: *Luciano in
Mickey Mouse
costume at a charity
dinner.*

Above: *Luciano with his wife, Adua.*

Right: *with his wife and daughters Giuliana, Christina and Lorenza.*

The poster from Pavarotti's début in La Bohème at the
Teatro Municipale in Reggio Emilia on April 29, 1961.

ENAL   CITTA' DI REGGIO NELL' EMILIA   ENAL

TEATRO MUNICIPALE

"PREMIO ACHILLE PERI,,

Direttore artistico ETTORE CAMPOGALLIANI

Sabato 29 aprile 1961   **Ore 21,15 precise**

Inaugurazione della Stagione Lirica ' Giovani Cantanti '

IN SERATA DI GALA

con la rappresentazione dell' opera

BOHÈME

Opera in 4 atti di G. GIACOSA e L. ILLICA
di GIACOMO PUCCINI

PERSONAGGI		INTERPRETI
RODOLFO	. . . .	LUCIANO PAVAROTTI
MARCELLO	. . .	VITO MATTIOLI
SCHANNARD	. . .	WALTER DE AMBROSIS
COLLINE	. . .	DMITRI NABOKOV
BENOIT	. .	
ALCIDORO	. . .	GUIDO PASELLA
MIMI'	. . .	ALBERTA PELLEGRINI
MUSETTA	. . .	BIANCA BELLESIA
PARPIGNOL	. .	A. PAVAROTTI
SERG. DOGANIERE	. . .	N. N.

MAESTRO DIRETTORE CONCERTATORE D'ORCHESTRA

FRANCESCO MOLINARI PRADELLI

Direttori del Coro   REGIA di   Maestro Suggeritore
GIANFRANCO MASINI   **MAFALDA FAVERO**   STELIO MAROLI
GAETANO RICCITELLI

ORCHESTRA E CORO DEL TEATRO MUNICIPALE

Capo macchinista : Osvaldo Tassani - Capo elettricista : Erio Camellini - Scene di Ercole Sormani - Costumi della Casa Imperia di Armando Arduino - Calzature Pedrazzoli - Parrucche Ditta Furioni.

Opposite page: *At La Scala in La Figlia del Reggimento, February 26, 1967.*

This page, top: *Pavarotti in a group photograph after the May 1961 production of* La Bohème *at the Teatro Comunale in Modena.*

Above, left: *with Mirella Freni in* I Puritani *in January 1969.* Centre: *with Mirella Freni in* L'Elisir d'amore *at La Scala on February 13, 1978.* Right: *on the twenty-fifth anniversary of his début, with Fiamma Izzo D'Amico in* La Bohème *at the Teatro Comunale in Modena, April 29,*

Opposite page:
Pavarotti thanks the audience after his recital at the Teatro Comunale in Modena on November 6, 1980.

This page, top: *three facial expressions during the 1986 Christmas concert at the Modena cathedral.*

Below: *during rehearsals for* La Bohème *in Modena on April 29, 1986.*

Right: *The Three Tenors with conductor Zubin Mehta after their concert at the Baths of Caracalla in Rome on July 6, 1990. Left to right: Placido Domingo, José Carreras, Mehta and Pavarotti.*

Below: *Pavarotti is presented to a bedraggled Prince and Princess of Wales after his concert in London's Hyde Park in July 1991.*

it is not so much he himself who produces art, but art and music that have used him. This makes Pavarotti happy in an almost childish way."

"What do you think is Pavarotti's relationship to his work?"

"Exactly that of someone who has been completely realised in his work, leaving him with a profound satisfaction. Pavarotti physically experiences a healthy pleasure that his pictures eloquently transmit."

"Pavarotti always smiles . . ."

"Because he shares his life with pleasure. A pleasure that becomes irony, jokes about himself, and humour. Pavarotti has fun whenever he can. Just take a look at his picture with William Wright, who helped him write his autobiography. He presents his book to the public with a towel over his shoulder and a cap on his head almost identical to the one he is wearing in the photo on the cover of the book. Through this sequence of images, he creates a playful, ironic game with his face, which appears three times in the same picture."

"Pavarotti has a very carnal quality."

"It's true. His gestures are always broad, decisive and fleshy, his hands seem to grasp, caress and model a shape. He is a man who is clearly immediate, whose psychological features are marked and linear, but who is also sudden and explosive. His bulk doesn't conceal an inner agility, an agility that can be seen in the mobility of his mimicry, in the continuous play of his being, his expression, his gestures, which reflect inner shifts that seem to follow each other rapidly, immediately, without intellectual mediation. There's something very significant about his picture with Sandro Pertini, the President of Italy. Both men are very spontaneous. No political ritual could falsify the deep, fraternal friendship between these two men, who feel that their success is the result of great commitment and attention to their work, and things other than themselves. When they met, they recognised in each other the same capacity to forget themselves in their work."

"Humanity is certainly one of Pavarotti's greatest characteristics."

"Yes, a humanity that moves from a joyous concept of life that extends to joking, to an absolutely intense concentration during a performance. Going through Pavarotti's photo albums you notice a succession of fast, almost violent changes that are always deeply sincere, since they always reflect a state of mind that seems real and actually experienced even in make-believe situations."

Professor Fanti concludes: "Reading these pictures I think I have come to understand that Pavarotti knows he can offer good music only by living in absolute honesty and in profound consistency with himself. You cannot pretend or cheat in the moment of singing, in the theatre. So for Pavarotti, theatrical make-believe becomes the key to opening and rediscovering the authentic side of himself. It shows us how something that often seems real to us, something in which we move and which we imagine to be real, becomes pretend, and how this allows a deeper investigation into the self, enabling Pavarotti to be very real on stage and truly real in the reality of life."

THE STAR'S CHART

I consult Gaudenzio Franceschini d'Eubach, an internation-
ally famed astrologer, in the hope that Pavarotti's horoscope
will help us understand something more than we will ever
learn from the official biographies and volumes written
about him. Pavarotti was born in Modena on 12 October 1935 at
one-thirty in the morning. According to an anecdote, his first
shouts (he didn't wail; he was already different from others at
birth) woke up the neighbours.

Born at that time, on that day, in that city, Pavarotti is a Libra,
with the sun in Libra, Mercury and Jupiter in Scorpio, Mars in
Sagittarius, Saturn in Pisces, the Moon in Aries, Uranus in
Taurus, Pluto in Cancer, Venus and Neptune in Virgo, and Leo
ascending. This may not mean much to amateurs, but it tells
astrologers a lot, despite the problems exposed by Piero Angela, a
popular figure on Italian television, and the author of several
serious scientific investigations, who told the television cameras
that astrology is for the simple-minded. But millions of people all
over the world believe in the stars. Ronald and Nancy Reagan
were reputed to have consulted a personal astrologer on a regular
basis. In fact, when the President of the United States and

Pavarotti met after a concert at Ford's Theater on March 20, 1981, they exchanged their opinions on the subject.

My first question is, "Mr. Franceschini, who is Luciano Pavarotti in astrological terms?"

"Pavarotti possesses lucidity and a great sense of justice, but he wishes to make profound analyses, he feels strong moral obligations, and he isn't self-indulgent, since he is also very self-critical. In the light of his ascendant, Leo, Luciano Pavarotti also appears strong, ambitious, courageous and sociable. He is sure of his own ideas, very proud, and expresses himself very frankly."

"They say that Pavarotti also has a certain admiration for himself."

"He certainly expresses a great charm, and his personality is tinged with a slight form of narcissism, but this is due more to his talent than to self-admiration."

"Does Pavarotti seek applause at all costs?"

"Let's say that he needs it. He often desires it to overcome a certain insecurity, and a certain feeling of loneliness."

"What are your auguries about Pavarotti and the crowds, the audiences."

"His emotional contacts with a crowd are much stronger than with a single person. The relationship that Pavarotti is able to establish with many people is immediate; he picks up their pulse easily, and can enchant them almost magically."

"What about Pavarotti and his feelings?"

"You can expect novel and unpredictable behaviour from him, but it is important to allow him his freedom and independence. He can create strong ties with those who share his interests, ideals, faith and even his illusions."

"It all adds up. Luciano and Adua Pavarotti form a couple beyond reproach. As far as illusions go, I find nothing to say. They know how to keep their feet on the ground, and you can tell," I say.

"Be careful: Pavarotti is cautious, but he can have an unpredictable attitude toward money. Even if he is quite logical, in certain moments he is highly quixotic, and can allow himself to be guided by inspirations that do not always prove to be positive. A discreet dose of luck helps him to get out of difficulties brilliantly."

"I have another question. Tell me about Pavarotti and the people."

"Pavarotti is very selective; he is a refined man who despises vulgarity. His contacts with people, with the most diverse groups, are guided by a strong personality and by frankness. He is a strong man, but he always has to feel like he's on the move. This hyperactivity could certainly bring him to the threshold of stress, because he doesn't allow himself to rest."

"They say that his intuitive abilities played a fundamental part in his career."

"He has a very profound, almost diabolical intelligence, with the ability to grasp situations immediately, and to make long-term plans."

"In fact, his calendar is booked up many years in advance. Yet Pavarotti is always smiling, available - at least that's the way he looks."

"He is a profoundly good man, but he is easily irritated and has a strong spirit of contradiction. He is also rather rebellious."

"What about Pavarotti and life?"

"His personality developed in a family environment marked by optimism. His horoscope says that he is very favoured in the acquisition of property."

You hardly need a horoscope to know that! Pavarotti has houses and villas. He knows how to invest his money. I return to my questions. "Pavarotti loves presenting himself as a tranquil man, doesn't he?"

"He's not completely tranquil," Franceschini asserts. "He has a healthy, somewhat explosive vitality. He alternates dynamism with calm."

"They say, 'Pavarotti, what an affectionate father'."

"He is. But sometimes his stance can be overbearing and a little pontifical. In any event his relationships are based more on friendship than on honey-coloured sentimentality. His relationships with his daughters have improved over the years, and now they communicate as equals. Moreover, Pavarotti is moving toward a greater stability in his affections and in sex."

"What can astrology tell us about Pavarotti's daily life?"

"He starts out patiently, but coldly eliminates any irritations that can get in the way of his career. He has a great capacity for work."

"Let's go back to Pavarotti's affections."

"In marriage he tends to restrain the expansion of his ego. He's afraid of being overly influenced, so he has his difficult moments. But Pavarotti often feels alone, although that's probably something he's chosen, in order to reach the goals he's set himself."

"Everyone says, 'Pavarotti, a great voice, but also a great businessman'."

"He is smart, but he can also be an opportunist. In short, he sees the big picture. He has one defect: he can be a little disorganised. I would suggest to him that he always seeks the advice of a good lawyer."

"You needn't worry. From what I know of Pavarotti and his wife, I think they've never wasted a penny. Is there fear of flying in his astrological chart?"

"You bet there is. But he would have flown anyway because he's very curious about every country in the world."

"How did Pavarotti realise himself?"

"His spirit of independence helped him a great deal. He trusted in his common sense, in his ability to say no, and naturally in his artistic skills. Then one day, the desire to be admired came into play, along with a slight form of exhibitionism. It was not enough to do him any harm, partly because of his histrionic talents, and the good feelings he releases."

"What do you think about Pavarotti and friendship?"

"His friendships are never new, but go back to his childhood and youth. He lives on friendships. He doesn't say so directly, but he often wants to be understood. If a friend disappoints him, he is deeply wounded; he can't stand solitude, even if he realises his maximum potential in solitude."

"Is there anything mysterious about Pavarotti's chart?"

"There certainly is! His vitality is drawn from unknown resources, especially in difficult moments. He is oriented toward mystery and the unusual."

"If you were a doctor rather than an astrologer, what would you advise him?"

"To stay on a diet. You don't need astrology to know that. It's in all the newspapers. He has to watch out for possible food poisoning, and he shouldn't be surprised if he gets a slight tachycardia. He might also have some minor problems with his eyesight."

"In short, as healthy as a horse."

"No, as healthy as Pavarotti."

A MEMO TO YOUNG
SINGERS

Opera fanatics say, "There will never be another Pavarotti." Nostalgic people who have put in their time, as Luciana Fusi called them, remember Di Stefano, Tebaldi, Callas and sigh: "Singers like those from our days aren't around any more." Other people say, "Italy is no longer the land of *bel canto* and beautiful voices; the tradition has migrated elsewhere." Still others add, "Too much business, too much politics between the notes . . . where will we end up?"

Luciano Pavarotti responds to this melancholy chorus with his optimism: "There are beautiful voices. We only need to look for them and train them."

The soprano Leyla Gencer, artistic and teaching director of Aslico, the Milanese school founded in the 1950's to prepare and launch young artists, notes: "I have realised that young singers today are more willing to study, more prepared, and more refined. Even if in general, for reasons I cannot explain, their voices have less in volume and strength than those in the earlier days."

The panorama is undoubtedly changing, which is why

Pavarotti created the International Competition, a tough audition that has brought before the footlights such major figures as Antonella Banaudi, who has been described as having "a rare voice, particularly suited for roles with strong dramatic tension." After her début at La Scala in 1987 in Verdi's *Nabucco* conducted by Riccardo Muti, Antonella Banaudi humbly took master classes with Carlo Bergonzi in Bussetto in the autumn of 1988, and won the international competition founded by Luciano Pavarotti.

In recent years Pavarotti seems to have decided to pay careful attention to young singers because his own early years were hard. Before achieving success he spent a long period of his life as a singer living in bohemian conditions. The conductor Richard Bonynge, who met Pavarotti in the early 1960s, describes him as pliant to direction and quick to grasp musical situations: "We all thought he sang marvellously from the start but, like all *real* singers, Luciano was never satisfied with himself and worked hard to improve his singing. He admired Joan's (Joan Sutherland) technique enormously. Every time I'd turn around, there he'd be with his hands on my wife's tummy trying to figure out how she supported her voice, how she breathed. Luciano is dead serious about singing and worked constantly to get better. He's continued to do so throughout his career."

In an interview with *Les Avants*, Bonynge revealed that in the days when the reality of performing in the United States was growing nearer, Pavarotti was afraid he wouldn't be able to keep up with the exhausting rhythm of work considered normal in its theatres. "But then he began to relax and enjoy the rigorous singing schedule, just as we all did. He was thrilled when, after singing 'Una furtiva lacrima' from *L'Elisir*, the audience made him sing it a second time, and then a *third* time. Pretty soon he would get upset if they didn't ask him to sing it three times."

Joan Sutherland has a special memory from those days: "The aspect of his voice that most struck us was its distinctive quality. If you hear a lovely voice but have no idea who is singing, it's just a sound. But with him, you knew immediately that it was Luciano singing."

Pavarotti once said: "To receive a rare gift like a great voice and then not fully develop it, or not use it in the best way possible, is in my opinion a serious crime. I have many venial sins on my conscience, but I'll be happy if I am judged innocent of this one, which I consider a mortal sin." The education of a singer, though, must necessarily pass through numerous obstacles. A singer can have a good voice, but not the character to confront difficulties. They may often be one step away from success only to slip silently into oblivion if their careers are not wisely managed.

If I had to describe Pavarotti, outside of pure musicianship, I would use the adjective 'wise'. He was wise in his initial choices, which he made after careful consideration; he has been wise in managing his voice, wise in his relationships with the opinion-makers and artistic directors. When Pavarotti embarked on the road to success he did so with an awareness and maturity beyond his years. The young Pavarotti who, as the protagonist of the opera *La Figlia del Reggimento*, The Daughter of the Regiment, was presented to the Queen Mother of England and Prince Philip on June 2, 1966, had nothing awkward about him, and showed no embarrassment. He handled the situation with ease and grace. The Queen Mother later said, "He won me over."

When Pavarotti remembers those years, he usually points out: "But it was hard. Nothing was easy. I knew how to smile, but inside I had to win many battles, especially my battle with fear." His difficulties naturally included being discovered, being picked out of the crowd by "someone". Newcomers don't have much choice.

In her interview with *Les Avants*, Sutherland made a harshly realistic observation: "There are very few real companies where young singers can settle down, work regularly, and learn their trade. Beginners must take whatever jobs are available. But in a way, the newcomers must share the blame for what's happening. They all want to be stars overnight. People like Caballé, Pavarotti and me - we all worked extremely hard for years before we got broad recognition. Caballé was singing away in Germany and

Switzerland for years, doing fantastic performances, I'm sure, and no one paid much attention.

"I was seven years at Covent Garden learning my trade. Pavarotti sang in smaller houses around Europe and in places like Miami and did gruelling work like our Australian tour. That tour didn't make him famous. But it was marvellous for him at that stage of his career because he was able to consolidate four big roles; later this stood him in good stead at the Met and other big houses."

In his early days Pavarotti thought it was enough to sing well, and give an approximation of the character. To William Wright who followed him around patiently for months with a tape-recorder, he confided: "When I started out, I was afraid that if I tried acting too much, it might look worse than trying very little. But I soon changed. I don't like doing anything badly, if I can improve. Also, I can't stay near anything too long without wanting to throw myself in it. I have worked very hard on my acting over the past fifteen years and I think I have made progress. Now I pay almost as much attention to the acting as to the singing."

Pavarotti has never forgotten how he started out, and can honestly say that he reached success without shoving people aside. He publicised his advice to young singers in the *Corriere della Sera*:

"I am often asked why I am interested in young artists, why, and for what reasons since January 1985 I have been trying to make my contribution to seeking out new voices and new talent. I could answer that it is a sentimental thing, that for me, an opera singer who has had everything he could desire, it is a moral commitment, a mission of sorts. But it is more than that, more than the desire to use my experience and my technical expertise in the service of the future.

"I would rather be practical and down-to-earth. This makes what I have to say much easier. We need young people, and I think it is only right that we open the way up to them. In this sense, helping them as best I can is a source of immense satisfaction. I have listened to hundreds of voices, travelled, and made innumerable contacts. And I feel good about that now, because good things have come out of it.

"There has been great progress in every sector of life and society. Compare how we live to the way people lived in the past. Science has worked miracles; what's happened in the fields of medicine, biology, information sciences and space research is wondrous. Art has been spread throughout the world, even to people who used to have no access to it. There seems to be nothing we can't do. Think of all the developments in recording music: here we are in the era of compact discs. Listening conditions when I started to sing were truly primitive by comparison.

"But opera singing faces many difficulties today, and the situation may have deteriorated by comparison to the past. It's true that there are many opportunities for young people, but there is also confusion. This is caused by the lack of real schools, and of what we could call the intermediate steps of a career. It used to be that a singer would spend a period of as many as three or four years in the provincial theatres. This was fundamental in preparing a singer for his or her transition to the bigger theatres. A career began at the provincial level, and then if someone had the right qualities, he or she would go on to national and international stages. We used to be terrified when we went to auditions. I remember that La Scala had one audition a year, and it was not easy to 'pass'. The people examining you were very demanding, and the competition was fierce.

"Now everything has changed. The demand for voices is so great that you immediately get thrown into the mix. There's no time to prepare yourself, and the risk of making mistakes is very great, which is why so many young talents end up burning out, and fail to live up to their promise. The competition that I've promoted all over the world is meant to remedy these organisational and artistic problems. After the European finals in Modena, the winners are taken to Philadelphia, where they are prepared for their début in the chosen operas. It's a long haul that concludes with the international finale. Even many of those who don't come in first accumulate a good deal of experience in the field that will enable them to face the future with better training.

"But aside from this commitment, I would like to give young singers some fatherly advice. They must learn to know themselves, and to know what their chances are. This is why they need two essential qualities: intelligence and humility. They must not take out their eventual frustrations on the audience or on the critics, but look inside themselves and try to understand why something happened. They must know the meaning of the word self-criticism.

"They must realise that singing is hard work, an investment in the future and not just a small venture to cash in on immediately. They must be perfectionists, but not maniacs, and realise that self-satisfaction is wrong. No one, not even the greatest singer, is born perfect. They must be wary of easy praise, and choose good teachers. Rather than listen to recordings by the great singers and try to imitate them, they should listen to themselves and see what they are doing right or wrong.

"They should try to understand what they are singing and believe in it. And they should also know how to wait: better a success in two years, I mean a true success, than an immediate, wasteful risk. Get to know the music, always study, never stop; these things are obvious, but they bear repeating. A beautiful voice is a gift, but you build up a profession one day at a time. Good examples of this come to us from many countries in the world, even the farthest away."

AND THEN HE
BECAME A DIRECTOR

In 1981, when Luciano Pavarotti decided to tell the story of his life in *Pavarotti, My Own Story*, every copy of which sold out long ago, he wrote: "I have no strong desire to direct an opera, but if I ever do, it will be a very literal interpretation, sticking to what I consider to be the composer's original intention. You will not see me trying to convert *Pelléas et Mélisande* into *Hair*, or *Rigoletto* into *The Elephant Man*."

Seven years later Pavarotti did decide to direct an opera. That summer, he ran into Gianni Tangucci, artistic director of the Teatro la Fenice in Venice, who asked him to return to the Serenissima for an opera of his own choosing. Pavarotti replied: "I'm ready to return, but not to sing. If you give me permission, I will direct a production." No sooner said than done. Tangucci and Pavarotti reached an agreement and decided on a new production of Donizetti's opera *La Favorita*, The Favourite. Pavarotti's *Favorita* would be a completely traditional staging.

The day before the opening, Pavarotti was as nervous as he had been on 29 April 1961, the day of his first *Bohème* in Reggio Emilia. He met with journalists and critics wearing an oversized red shirt from his pre-diet days, a handkerchief around his neck, and wrinkled trousers. Sandro Cappelletto of *La Stampa* who followed the rehearsals, described him as demanding and meticulous. At the press conference, Pavarotti appeared to be very humble.

When Ornella Rota of *La Stampa* asked him about his relationship with Beppe De Tomasi, a professional director, Pavarotti openly admitted: "He helped me, but he is a real director. He accepted out of friendship, out of the joy of being together." When she asked, "Is it harder to sing or to direct?" Pavarotti immediately responded: "To sing, no question about it. Because a director can decide by himself, based on his brain and on his ideas, while a singer always has to negotiate with his or her voice, and come to terms with it."

When the reporters asked Pavarotti what his *Favorita* would be like, he repeated the words he had uttered many years before: "The first requirement is to serve the music and the singers with the greatest fidelity and care. So I avoided cuts as much as possible. I worked within the traditional framework, without trying experiments that would have been unconvincing; only one small variant is planned, with the Queen of Spain, in the opera's finale."

Pavarotti is never stingy with praise for his co-workers, and to Claudio Pasqualetto of *Corriere della Sera* he confided: "I couldn't have found a better cast, beginning with the protagonist, Shirley Verret, a professional with a great personality. If you start out at such a high level everything has to go well." But after thinking it over, when Ornella Rota asked him, "Are you worried about opening night?" Pavarotti confessed: "Yes, very much. I'm almost sure I am going to be booed, but whatever happens, that's the risk you run in this profession."

Despite all this, he described the atmosphere in the theatre as calm, with everyone working together enthusiastically, as a team. But there were some unknown factors. "In a performance, in any performance, even the most insignificant detail can turn against its creator." What was Pavarotti afraid of? Expectations ran high, but they were full of good will. The production was

traditional, and the cast was first rate. Yet the critical conscious-
ness that has accompanied him throughout his career also
emerged on this occasion, and before the curtain rose Luciano
declared that this would be the last time he would ever direct.
"This will be the first and last time, whether it goes well or
poorly. I did it out of curiosity, to see what happens on the other
side, and what kind of problems a director has."

The future would reveal whether all this was meant to ward
off bad luck, or was so much word-play. Curiosity was certainly
a factor: his desire to test how the relationship between director
and singer is created undoubtedly played a large part in putting
Pavarotti on the other side of the pit. He also may have wanted to
settle a score with a director that dated from twenty years earlier
in the United States.

Ornella Rota dug deeper into the new relationship between
Pavarotti and opera when she asked, "What effect does it have on
you to direct Fernando, a role you performed many times?" The
tenor assured her, "I'm happy to be doing it, and I feel close to the
man who is singing this most difficult, impracticable part." Pietro Ballo, the tenor, did not disappoint him, and was a big
success.

Pavarotti was even more cautious with Roberta Pasero of *Il
Giornale*: "I enjoy being the director, but for the moment I'm
going to hold off shouting 'Victory', which I never did even when
I really was a winner in my career. For now I am waiting for
opening night." He explained: "I belong to the generation that
saw the war. I was a child, but every day I learned that nothing
came easy. I learned from my father and my mother that you had
to keep on moving, whatever it cost. My feeling like a pioneer,
always wanting to do something new and extravagant, probably
dates back to that period."

Furthermore: "However things go, when I go back to the
other side of the barricades the experience will help me to be
more co-operative with directors, with the real directors. Are
there few of them? It's not for me to say. There are not many
tenors or baritones, either, and maybe that's why they pay us so

well." When Ms Pasero asked for his opinion of directors and production styles he answered with some irritation: "I am bothered by big theatres that contract famous directors because they know that their provocative productions will attract popular and critical attention."

Clearly Pavarotti has not forgotten the time he was singing the role of Fernando in a big American company. The director of *La Favorita* held a press conference, and when a critic asked him how things were going, he replied, "We are doing the best we can, considering Mr Pavarotti's acting."

In *Pavarotti: My Own Story*, the tenor recalls this unpleasant day: "This made me very angry. I have performed that part all over the world with great critical acclaim for my dramatic characterisation. In a sense, he was announcing ahead of time to the critics what they should think of my acting. It was a betrayal and very unfair. I protested to the management. I calmed down, we worked it out, but for a while I didn't want to go through with the performances."

Later in the same chapter Pavarotti presents his "manifesto", or rather what he considers the proper philosophical approach to directing an opera. In his production at La Fenice, he remained faithful to this philosophy: "There are many very talented directors working in opera today - Ponnelle is certainly one of them - men with interesting visions of what the operas should be, visions of how to make us see the operas in a new way. In these matters, however, I lean toward conservatism. Sometimes the changes and additions take the work so far from the original that it ceases to be a matter of interpretation and becomes rewriting. It is almost as though the director was embarrassed by the opera for having been written in the nineteenth century, and seeks to disguise it so we won't recognise it. Sometimes, too, these radical productions are simply a matter of ego: the directors don't want to present Verdi or Puccini, they want to present themselves.

"I think the people who do new, avant-garde productions should be careful about taking bows *before* the event. So often in New York or elsewhere, you see the creators - the director and the conductor, perhaps some of the singers - going on television to congratulate themselves about their new concept. They talk on and on about how they discovered hidden values and shades of undiscovered meaning in a familiar opera. Everyone gets as excited as *they* seem to be. Then it opens and what do you have? Just another *Traviata* or *Rigoletto* - perhaps not even a good one."

The day before the opening night of *La Favorita*, when Ornella Rota asked him what the ideal opera director should be like, Pavarotti hadn't changed his mind. "He must have ideas and be a good co-ordinator. He must do everything in such a way that it is believable. It's anything but easy." She ventured, "Is there anything you would like to tell opera directors?" Pavarotti responded with a joke. "I have nothing to say. I'm a singer who at a certain point in his life decided, for the sake of personal satisfaction, to direct an opera." Rota insisted, "And if you were a singer working with Pavarotti the director, what would you tell him?" "I would thank him."

On the night of 23 December 1988, the curtain rose on Pavarotti's production of *La Favorita*. He was tense, but didn't show it to anyone. His duty that night as director was to give other people confidence, which he did. The opera was a success. The first words of praise came out the next day from Dino Villatico, a critic for *La Repubblica*. His words were addressed to the tenor-director in particular.

"Luciano Pavarotti's touch can be felt especially in the care each singer took to pronounce the text they were singing clearly and distinctly. In this way we can finally see a performance in which voice is a theatrical means, and not a gymnasium of individual exhibitions. Among other things, the clarity of the diction also makes you better appreciate the beauty of the melodies. Not only that: with this type of interpretation, Pavarotti demonstrates that making yourself understood when you sing is not impossible. If singers don't do it, it's because they don't want to do it. Having restored his voice to its theatrical function, Pavarotti also strips down the repertory of gestures to which singers on stage usually abandon themselves. He saves only a few, and uses them just enough to show what a character says or feels. He strives for a certain balance between the emphatic conventionality of operatic gesture and the narrative clarity that gesture must possess in a modern performance. The effect is very clean, with movements that allow the necessary space for musical expression."

But there was one small mishap during the performance. When in the third act Fernando furiously pulls out his sword before the king, it came out of its scabbard folded in two, bent at the point where it was later supposed to break. A tense Pavarotti worried that laughter would stop the singers. Instead, the tension was so great that the audience didn't breathe. At the end, Pavarotti the director was showered with applause. The reporter from *Il Resto del Carlino* described his appearance at show's end as, "Face sweating and tense, huge in his red sweater." Pavarotti admitted he hadn't slept for several nights.

De Tomasi, the assistant director (but Pavarotti repeatedly stated: "He's the real director, I have to say"), commented: "Luciano worked mainly with the singers, I suggested some ideas, provided some technical assistance, in places where a beginner would not know what to do. But Luciano is so good that with his next production, I'm sure he'll be stealing my job."

The mezzo-soprano Shirley Verret, who won great applause, remembers: "I sang *Favorita* at the Met with Luciano thirteen years ago. He understands the problems of operas and singers. Yes, there are directors who do grandiose things, for effect, but then they impose absurd things on you. Ronconi is a great director, and I sang in his *Mosè* at the Paris Opera, but he pays no attention to the singers, his ideas don't include us. With Luciano it was very restful. You feel supported. It's wonderful. I accepted this *Favorita* in Venice during the Christmas period for Luciano. Usually I'm at home for Christmas, but this time I made my husband and daughter come to me."

Pietro Ballo, the tenor, adds: "Pavarotti made me understand my part as no one else could have. He also taught me how to control my breathing, sing in the right position, and reserve myself where I could, in order to be in prime shape for the aria 'Spirito gentil' in the fourth act. He made everything easier. He also created a great work environment."

The following day, Mario Pasi of the _Corriere della Sera_, who was more cautious in his praise, pointed out, "Pavarotti was right to acknowledge the help he received from Beppe De Tomasi, who has staged _La Favorita_ many times in different theatres over the years. In this way, he was able to focus his attention on the singers, guiding them to find the right expression and to respect the demands of this difficult score. The result is a traditional, deliberately nineteenth-century production: no innovative temptations here, but total respect for the opera."

Dino Tonon wrote in _Il Giornale_: "This _Favorita_ is a version mainly interpreted to give room to the singers. Everyone on stage moved with great assurance: the great Shirley Verret, the bass Roberto Scanduzzi, the tenor Pietro Ballo, Paolo Coni and Daniela Mazzuccato. You could see the work Pavarotti had done to find the right gestures and movements to place the singers at their ease."

Pavarotti followed his _Favorita_ from a box, and the day after the opening, at the press conference, he told Sandro Cappelletto of _La Stampa_: "I tried to see the opera as a member of the audience, but I have to admit it wasn't much fun, I was too nervous. Why should I lie?"

BECOMING A
LEGEND

On 16 January 1988 Pavarotti became a legend. Exactly twenty-seven years had gone by since his début in Reggio Emilia, when a headline in the *Corriere della Sera* referred to him and his tour of China as "legendary". The night before in New York a documentary film, or rather a travelogue, called *Distant Harmony* was screened. The film, directed by DeWitt Savage, was about the tour Pavarotti made in and around Beijing and it provoked the "legendary" headline from the Italian newspaper.

Pavarotti explained the circumstances to the New York journalists: "We were one of the first companies in the world to go to China to present an Italian opera. I was ready for any kind of reaction, from the most caustic to enthusiastic. We were very lucky. They gave us the best welcome you can imagine. The Chinese went wild. What a wonderful, big surprise to see them so excited and warm-hearted, and what a privilege to be the first opera singer to enter the "Great House of the People". Before a wild crowd of ten thousand people we wrote a page of history. The speech I gave after the concert was not prepared, but came from the bottom of my heart. Music is international, and does not need translation, but more than anything else it is a message of peace."

With his trip to China Pavarotti reached one of the peaks of his career, and the days he spent in Beijing made him reflect on his life up to that moment. What obstacles had he had to overcome to achieve his goals, one after the other, and through what highways and byways did his "artistic engineering" unwind? In New York Pavarotti took another long look at his life, and realised that in the chess tournaments of the big theatres, he had played his game well.

From the beginning, every step he made was carefully considered. Less than a year after the applause in Reggio Emilia, he was already on his way to his first foreign engagement, and appeared at the National Theatre of Belgrade in *La Traviata*, The Fallen Woman. Then in rapid succession came Amsterdam, the Staatsoper of Vienna, and Dublin. Before he could finally win over the international public, however, he needed the approval of the United States. He set his sights on New York, and the Metropolitan Opera became his chief goal.

But first he had to settle a score with Milan. Despite his numerous successes in Italy and abroad, La Scala continued to shut its door in his face. Luciano felt as if they were treating him high-handedly. These were difficult days, and they left a bitter taste. Some years later he would tell William Wright: "When I was finally contracted to sing at La Scala, it was not, I am sorry to say, because of any enthusiasm towards me on the part of the management at that opera house. Although I had not performed at La Scala the directors knew me and my singing. At that time La Scala had a reciprocal arrangement with the Vienna Opera to supply singers - speranzi or young hopefuls - in emergencies. I would often be sent up to cover for their tenors. Though they were in no hurry to have me sing on their own stage, the La Scala management didn't mind sending me to sing on Vienna's."

Pavarotti would reach La Scala on 28 April 1965 in *La Bohème* under the baton of von Karajan. Assistance came from an unexpected quarter.

Joan Ingpen was the Controller of Opera Planning at the Royal Opera House, Covent Garden. It was her job to choose singers for the London house. On 27 May she went to hear *Rigoletto* at the Gaiety Theatre in Dublin, hardly in the best of moods. She had contracted Giuseppe Di Stefano to sing in *La Bohème* at Covent Garden, but she knew he wasn't always reliable, and was capable of cancelling an engagement at the last minute. She had to find a cover in order to prevent a managerial flop. The laws of opera are ruthless, as anyone who has fallen foul of them can testify. The Pavarotti whom she saw walking across the stage of the Gaiety Theatre in the role of the Duke of Mantua seemed awkward, and played too much to the gallery, "hanging on to his high notes as if he would never let go," but with a "fantastic" voice.

Joan Ingpen thought Pavarotti would make a good standby replacement for Giuseppe Di Stefano, so she consulted with a few experts. One of them launched into a merciless criticism: "Pavarotti doesn't know how to move, on stage he seems overcome by embarrassment, and seems obsessed by the thought 'should I put my hands this way or this way'." This could have been an irrevocable verdict, but Ingpen went to Pavarotti anyway with some straight talk: not too much money, only the last performance, unless Di Stefano cancelled, and some acting lessons as a prerequisite. Pavarotti accepted, and actually arrived in London a few days before he was due. He prepared carefully, and waited for his chance. He was right to wait, and his patience was rewarded. Di Stefano sang on opening night, but stopped halfway through the second performance and left. With Pavarotti the atmosphere in the theatre warmed up. This was his true international baptism, and from that day on the tenor would be one of London's best-loved stars.

Another woman paved the way for his triumphs in the United States: Joan Sutherland, the great soprano, a tall woman who was always having problems with tenors who were not her height. Ingpen, who knew all the backstage news of the entertainment world, immediately realised that Pavarotti would be a perfect partner for Sutherland. She picked up the telephone, called the singer's manager-husband Richard Bonynge, and shouted into the receiver: "This time I've found him, and he's as tall as Joan wants." A few days later a long-lasting association began. In his interview with *Les Avants* some years later, Bonynge would say: "Pavarotti has the kind of voice that comes along once in a century."

Sutherland and Bonynge decided to have Luciano début in Miami in *Lucia di Lammermoor*, and together they gave him some extra training. He had expressed some initial doubts the day they proposed a long tour in Australia, to sing in Sydney, Melbourne, Adelaide and Brisbane. In July 1965, in the course of a few days Pavarotti would sing *L'Elisir d'Amore*, *La Traviata*, *Lucia di Lammermoor* and *La Sonnambula*, shifting from Nemorino's costume to Alfredo's, from Edgardo's to Elvino's. It was a long hot summer, but one that would pay off. In December La Scala invited him to appear for the second time, and almost rolled out the red carpet. With *Rigoletto* he finally had a triumph at La Scala.

Now, though there were no more obstacles in his path, there was still one thing shadowing Pavarotti. He had travelled the world like a refugee before receiving money and recognition in Italy but his great love for Modena was not reciprocated. Later he would openly discuss his relationship to his hometown with Wright. "The city in which I was born and raised never gave me the least encouragement." He explained that shortly after his début in Reggio Emilia, he offered himself to the Teatro Comunale of Modena. He was told he couldn't be given the part because the managers didn't consider him reliable enough.

Luciano has observed: "Still there is a curious antagonism between the cities and the native sons who try for international fame and glory. The touchiness exists, I am sure, on both sides." Basically, you have to try to understand the people of Modena. They consider that they have no equals in the world. One person who noticed this was Paul Newman, the very private American star whom many people would love to see up close. When he came to Modena for the first time to buy a Ferrari, he stopped at Fini's for lunch. No one asked him for an autograph. Before leaving, the actor mentioned to his friends, "What a polite city - no one bothered me." When he returned to Modena, he dined at La Fazenda, and the same thing happened. This time Paul Newman was not happy. He felt like a stranger in a strange land. "To interest the people of Modena, who do you have to be?" he asked.

Pavarotti's success grew from day to day. In January 1967 he met the conductor Herbert von Karajan a second time, for a concert commemorating the tenth anniversary of Arturo Toscanini's death. Now he knew he had arrived, but the conquest of America was still before him.

FROM AMERICA
TO CHINA

Today, twenty-five years later, some people wonder if Luciano Pavarotti discovered America or if America discovered Pavarotti. Both are probably true. In the United States the tenor certainly found the most congenial habitat for achieving celebrity, but there are those who maintain that Pavarotti allowed himself to be devoured by the Americans. The most recent evidence, however, proves that Pavarotti was able to manage and dominate the greatest consumer market in the world, without compromising his artistic and human personality.

An Italian-American director, Anthony Stivanello, helped him get his foot in the door. In Miami in October 1965, Pavarotti was preparing to face the public in *Lucia di Lammermoor*, on Sutherland's invitation, but Stivanello convinced him that his acting was not up to the level of his singing. Pavarotti accepted the criticism, and the two holed up in a hotel, going over the movements for days. Luciano confessed one of his troubles to Stivanello: he was still thinking about a bad review he received from a nasty critic: "Pavarotti never broke character. How could he? He never entered into the character." Moreover there was

Sutherland's advice: "It's not enough to sing a part - you also have to act it." After Australia and La Scala, here, at last, was the United States. But suddenly he was assailed by doubts, uncertainties, and perplexities. What Pavarotti wouldn't have given to return to sceptical Modena. But instead his American début was a triumph; in Miami he graduated with a "first". This opened the way to Pavarotti's final goal: the Metropolitan Opera House in New York.

Pavarotti first came to New York in the autumn of 1967 to cover for Carlo Bergonzi in Verdi's *Requiem*, but he got a bad impression of the city: rude people, dirty and oppressive skyscrapers that seemed to shut out the sky, the sense that personality was erased: an unliveable place, all in all. Later he would change his mind, and discover the city's true character. He would make the friends he needed, and have his greatest successes in New York.

In November 1968 he returned to the American stage in San Francisco, in *La Bohème*. It was a complete success, and one that would be noticed as far away as New York by Sir Rudolf Bing, director of the Metropolitan Opera. Luciano told a friend, "I feel like Daniel in the lions' den." He was not all wrong. Amid the all-pervasive enthusiasm of the public, he could feel a tinge of sadism, and the critics seemed willing to dip their pens in poison. When the Met was within reach, fortune seems to have suddenly turned its back on Luciano. On the eve of his début he came down with a bad case of influenza, and was terrified that no one would believe he was truly indisposed. Pavarotti worried, "They'll think I'm running away, that fear got the better of me, that I chickened out."

He would later confirm this to Wright: "New York is so sceptical that nothing less than the sight of my dead body laid out in Lincoln Center Plaza would have convinced the public that I really did have the Hong Kong flu." Luckily his childhood friend Mirella Freni was in New York in those days, and scheduled to sing at the Met with him. She wanted to help him, but at the same time was terrified of catching the flu from him. She prepared boiling-hot minestrone, cautiously approached his dressing-room door, and ran away whispering, "*Povero amico mio, povero ragazzo*. My poor friend, poor boy!" It was like a scene from *La Bohème* with the roles reversed: a dashing Mimì and a dying Rodolfo.

Pavarotti wanted to go home to Italy, but instead made a compromise with Sir Rudolf Bing: his début would be postponed for a week in the hope that he would get over his flu. On November 23 he had to decide: Pavarotti met with Rudolf Bing in a rehearsal room at the Met and tried a few passages from *La Bohème*. Sir Rudolf decided they could go ahead with the début, and Pavarotti appeared at the dress rehearsal, dejected and disheartened. Only Mirella seemed affectionately close to him, while the conductor, Molinari Pradella, was incomprehensibly and decidedly hostile.

Pavarotti would say, "He could have helped me - giving a strong phrase in a weak spot, allowing me to breathe, anticipating trouble, and other technical matters, but his baton was inflexible." In his autobiography Pavarotti would attack conductors like Molinari Pradella: "There is a certain kind of conductor who works only for himself and his vision of the music. He is getting his direction from On High and regards the singer, if he regards him at all, as another one of his obedient instruments. It is very demoralising to look down from the stage and see that the person you are relying on to get you through cares not at all if you live or die. This dependence of singers on conductors is always true, but particularly so when you feel dreadful and are not in voice."

But singing by Luciano's side was Mirella Freni, acting as his sister, friend and mother. Throughout the opera she whispered words of encouragement, and with God's help he made it to the end. Pavarotti waited by a newstand for the first reviews to come in, and breathed a sigh of relief when he read Peter Davis, music critic for the *New York Times*: "Mr Pavarotti triumphed principally through the natural beauty of his voice - a bright, open instrument with a nice metallic ping up top that warms into an even, burnished lustre in mid-range. Any tenor who can toss off high C's with such abandon, successfully negotiate delicate diminuendo effects and attack Puccinian phrases so fervently is going to win over any *La Bohème* audience and Mr Pavarotti had them eating out of his hand."

However, Pavarotti could not make it through the next performance, and had to quit after the second act. All he wanted was to go back to Modena as quickly as possible. He went to bed, and locked himself in the house for three months. He was a wreck, regretting he had not become an insurance agent or school teacher. It was as if the praise he had received in half the world had never existed. A veil had descended between Luciano and reality that would not be raised until two months later, when he returned to the stage in *La Bohème* at La Scala in Milan. It would be another two years before the tenor would set foot on an American stage again. He started back in San Francisco with his début opera, but would not return to the Met until October 1970, with *Lucia di Lammermoor* and *La Traviata*. His crowning success there would be in 1972, when he sang *La Figlia del Reggimento* with Joan Sutherland.

One of Pavarotti's agents, Herbert Breslin, has described that moment; how it was made even more special considering the difficulty in winning over New Yorkers. But Pavarotti succeeded, "singing like a god". Breslin recalls: "At each performance he stopped the show with those nine high C's in one aria. He didn't rely solely on his singing. He acted the role wonderfully, too, throwing himself into a zesty, comic characterisation."

The rest followed naturally: the great concerts, the television recitals, riding horseback as Grand Marshal of the Columbus Day parade, and the warm embrace at parade's end by the then President of the United States, Jimmy Carter. Pavarotti's popularity in the United States soared and has continued to soar, making him perhaps the most popular personality in the United States today. To those who say Pavarotti has handed himself over, body and soul, to the mass media, Breslin replies: "Luciano knows what he's doing, and what he's doing is good for opera. At any rate he has proven that a great singer can be a charming human being, and not just an unavailable personality locked in an ivory tower."

So where else but New York could Pavarotti première the documentary film of his tour of China? After the screening Pavarotti told reporters, "This is extremely satisfying, but in China I realised that you can always learn something more." When Alessandra Farkas of the *Corriere della Sera* asked him, "What did you learn?" Pavarotti replied: "A little Chinese philosophy, which was a pleasant surprise because it's so similar to the way the Italian philosophy used to be. The Chinese people resemble the Italy of when I was a boy. They aren't rich, but they're full of smiles and joy. After the war, we too had a great desire to laugh. We played in the streets every night under the lamp-posts, got around by bicycle, and used horses as a means of transportation, as the Chinese do today. I stopped biking when I was twenty-five, after I bought my first car."

In the documentary you see Pavarotti on a bicycle, light as a feather, going down the streets of Beijing. Many viewers have wondered why in every scene he wears a big, colourful *foulard*. Luciano explains: "I bought a *foulard* made out of cashmere and silk for the women at home, but it was so beautiful I couldn't separate myself from it. It's a fabulous protection. It shelters me from the cold and from the heat, and is maybe a little like my Linus blanket. Naturally it's red, because red is my favourite colour, the one that best reflects my personality."

PAVAROTTI ON
PAVAROTTI

W hat about "King Pavarotti"? *The Corriere della Sera* declared him a legend, but on February 7, 1989, the *Resto del Carlino* crowned him with a full-page headline, "Pavarotti enthroned", after the première of Verdi's opera *Un ballo in Maschera*, A Masked Ball, in Bologna.

The music critic, Adriano Cavicchi, paid him such a high tribute for the following reason: "Never before has such an amazing consensus been given at the première of an opera by Verdi. Luciano Pavarotti appeared in excellent form, and was able to suggest expressive, dramatic depth with remarkable flexibility and fidelity to his character's twisting states of mind. His portrayal of the character of Riccardo was peerless, because of his ability to give the role the tantalising vocal flights that idealise the urgency of an uncontrollable passion. Pavarotti's interpretative style created many moments of startling elegance. One of the finest moments was the famous 'O come fa da ridere', in which his laughter was tinged with a barely audible shudder, communicating both his outward mockery of the dreadful prophecy, and his palpable anxiety, almost a repressed terror."

When the final curtain fell, Pavarotti jumped for joy, "like a football fan", according to Carlo Fontana, director of the Teatro Comunale of Bologna.

Valeria Vicari, on special assignment for the *Carlino*, wrote: "Luciano Pavarotti, the great sovereign - risk-taker and joker, elegant and chivalric, ready to throw himself into his passions or to renounce them, tragic in the opera's dramatic moments - showed up for his press conference as happy as a boy, and he asked the questions. He was available, and signed autographs, receiving mobs of people. 'How were we? Did you have a good time? What did you like better, *Trovatore* or *Ballo*?' "

Vicari asked him, "There were thirty minutes of applause for your *Trovatore* in America; was your reception on this side of the ocean warmer?"

"It was the same," Pavarotti replied. "You can see for yourself. I feel as if the Riccardo character were sewn on top of me vocally and dramatically. If I had to choose a role to show off my powers, this would be the one."

The next day, under the headline "The Return of a Star", Paolo Gallarati of *La Stampa* wrote: "The artistic director of the Bologna theatre succeeded in surrounding the *divo* - who has fortunately never acted like a true *divo* - with a company that was up to the task. This was no easy task, considering that even after his long career, nature still supplies the great Luciano with the absolute fullness of his vocal equipment and the steady temperament that is a model for generations of young singers who wish to specialise in the difficult art of Italian opera."

"I wish I could sing it for the rest of my life," Pavarotti told Domizia Carafoli of the *Giornale* after the performance. She used this statement for the title of her article, which was dedicated almost exclusively to Pavarotti. She wrote: "Yes, it's true, the party was for him. In *Ballo in Maschera* Luciano Pavarotti stole everyone's hearts, and eliciting teardrops, heartbeats, sighs, sobs, passions and ecstasy. All this for him, dressed up as King Gustavo III of Sweden and looking like a guru in his long velvet gown, which was purple in defiance of every superstition. He looked toward the sky amid the tumult of applause, joined his hands, and opened his arms wide to grasp his fans in an ecumenical hug. A heady cocktail of enthusiasm and devotion that turned the evening into 'Pavarotti night', making everyone forget that the whole production was top quality, even without the tenor.

"The radiant Pavarotti, who is still unequalled and untouchable at the ripe age of fifty-three, sang the love duet with Amelia with such ease and elegance that the audience forgot the piece's technical and vocal difficulties, so natural was his tenderness and desperation, climbing irresistibly to the final top note. The uncontrollable enthusiasm of the audience forced the conductor, Gustav Kuhn, to take a seemingly interminable pause."

The day after Pavarotti's triumph, I went to see him in Saliceta San Giuliano. The happiness that Valeria Vicari had observed a few hours earlier was still on him, like a second skin. He hugged me, saying "I'm happy."

In the box office it's a day like any other: Adua is on the telephone non-stop taking care of her singers, to whom she administers the same wisdom she dedicates to her husband. Francesca, the office manager, is busy with the computer, schedules and accounts. She also has to handle the requests arriving from all over the world. Everyone wants Pavarotti, and Adua repeats almost obsessively: "I'm sorry, but Luciano is booked until 1992."

Those who really want him try for 1993. "The next time I come by I'll bring you a 1993 calendar," I joke. "That's exactly what I need," she says. "I'll print a single copy for you," I promise.

Luciano takes me by the arm, and the two wolfhounds, which I'm told are almost ferocious, dance around us festively. For once the master is home. They deserve some attention too. This is where his love for animals began, in a conversation with Vittorio Emiliani, who asked him a few years ago about his future plans.

Luciano replied: "On the four hectares I bought here in Saliceta San Giuliano, I would like to bring my four horses, and personally supervise their grooming. Now I keep them at a stable. I'm a horse fanatic. Horses court each other like human beings, following each other around as if they wanted to kiss." Pavarotti says: "Horses had an important place in my childhood, maybe because when I was a boy I used to visit an uncle who lived near the market. Every Monday it was a zoo, a fascinating show. He kept his horses on viale Storchi, where today all you find are garages and cars. The smell of petrol has replaced the smell of the fields. Maybe we have forgotten that the horse was a great companion to man. It shared in all our labours, making them easier.

"I also want to plant some new trees. Once upon a time four hectares could produce enough for a family to live on, as long as the ground was cultivated. We would be happy to keep up the garden, without overdoing it. I hope I can continue this way. I think of these things not for the distant future, but for a deferred present."

Pavarotti's memories are simple, and the applause of the great theatres seems far away. I tell him: "Now you seem defenceless and unarmed, but it took real grit to get you where you are today; I think it takes more than a voice to have a career like yours." Pavarotti replies: "It wasn't so much grit as will power. Maybe it's true that I seem defenceless, but who am I supposed to defend myself against? Everyone likes me." This is indeed his greatest achievement, rivalling all the applause showered on him. But William Wright found out how willing Pavarotti was to expose himself to criticism the day they teamed up to write his autobiography. "Highlight the difficult moments of my career, the negative aspects of my personality," Pavarotti told him.

I remind him of this quotation. "Luciano," I ask, "would you have me believe you are a masochist?"

"Absolutely not. I made that request because in the long run, our negative sides are what makes us human. Everyone thinks that an opera singer is a privileged creature. I wouldn't deny this, but there are still dues to pay."

"Everyone says, 'Pavarotti is a good person, and not just a great tenor.' But I'm sure you've been bad sometimes too."

"I'm normal, and not so much good as understanding. But what do you mean by being good or bad?"

"Is there anything you regret having done?"

"We all make the mistake of thinking that we don't have to apologise to anyone when we're adults. This is wrong. I'm always apologising. But I don't think I'm ever unkind."

"Who have you apologised to?"

"I don't remember."

"How do you imagine the public?"

"The public is the people. I try to give my profession, what I've studied, and what I know to the public. I try to share all this with people. This is what the public is to me, nothing more."

"Does an opera singer do a job or perform an art?"

"A little of both, because a singer doesn't create, but does something that should be the same for everyone. 'Che gelida manina' is an aria that all tenors should sing in the same way. Only the interpretation changes."

"Let's talk about your diction. Critics say that it is as important as a good voice. Your father's diction is also perfect. Did you inherit yours from him?"

"Evidently. Opera voices that express sweetness tend toward good pronunciation, otherwise no one would appreciate them."

"You once said, 'In the summer of 1965 I knew I had a voice, but I didn't feel I had mastered it yet'. When did you set aside those doubts?"

"They weren't just doubts. I only felt like the complete master of my voice after I had been singing for ten years."

"You once confessed that your relations with La Scala were difficult."

"I don't think relations with La Scala have been easy for anyone, because that theatre is always a testing ground. You can never feel completely safe, so things go in unexpected directions. It depends on how the production is put together. La Scala is like a beautiful woman - it always makes you anxious."

"Why are you so superstitious?"

"Our profession is so difficult that it becomes a kind of religion, a god of sorts. I hope this doesn't sound blasphemous."

"What is your theory on the tenor's voice?"

"My theories are borrowed from the past, from my predecessors. I have nothing new to add."

"What is the *do di petto*, the high C with full voice?"

"It's a note that can probably be compared to the goal in a soccer game. If it's there, so much the better. But you can also play well without scoring a goal."

"You've had many triumphs and much applause, but you were also panned by *Time* magazine in 1981 after singing in Verdi's *Aïda* in San Francisco."

"I don't remember. Maybe . . . but it was a good *Aïda*. I follow the critics, read them, and immediately take note of what they say. In general I don't forget them. But if you say that in 1981 *Time* magazine . . . I suppose it's true."

"And in 1982, when you were supposed to sing in *Idomeneo* and *Tosca*, the performances were cancelled because you were 'allergic to stage dust'. Not everyone believed you, and some reporters invented all kinds of stories."

"The truth is that I had a bad allergy that was hard to understand and cure. Then they discovered it was horses. Anywhere I went, in Italy or in other parts of the world, I would come down with these allergy attacks. During that time, in memory of my childhood days, I grew fond of horses and started going to stables in every city I visited. At the beginning I didn't make the connection, which is why that story about an allergy to stage dust came about. I was really allergic to the dust in stables, around horses. It got into my throat, and almost immediately made my voice go."

"How did you get better?"

"By staying away from horses."

"Was it a big sacrifice?"

"Yes, extremely."

"Now you seem to be much better."

"Yes, let's hope it lasts."

"How many horses do you own?"

"Four colts, two mares and two stallions."

"Luciano, do you remember the time you were booed at La Scala in *Lucia di Lammermoor*?"

"I'll never forget it."

"What happened?"

"I messed up the last ten or twelve bars, the hardest ones in the opera. I offered my side."

"Considering the great singing you had already done, don't you think the audience could have been a little more generous?"

"In opera what you did the day before doesn't matter. And at La Scala you always have to prove yourself. As Eduardo said, 'The exams are never over'."

"How did you react?"

"I took note of it. I didn't get mad at the audience, or at the critics, who blew the whole thing totally out of proportion. I took it with philosophy and bitterness. I thought to myself, 'Let's hope this doesn't happen again'. The other nights went much better."

"Weren't those boos a little small-minded?"

"I'm not the person you should ask. You should ask the people who were doing the booing, and the critics who wrote those terrible reviews. Please don't ask me to call someone else a rotten scoundrel. If someone acts like a rat, that's the way they should feel, without having to be told."

"How do you get along with the critics?"

"Fine. We've always got along great. By critics I mean ninety per cent of them, because there are another ten per cent that are always against you. I already know what they're going to write before it comes out. What's more, I could write some articles even before they do."

"It has been said that 'Pavarotti is the last great opera singer'."

"The same was said in the past about other singers. It's simply not true. Every year brings new talent."

"But it's also true that no important new voices have emerged for a few years now."

"Not quite. Some important voices have appeared, but they haven't perfected their technique."

"Why?"

"Because they aren't put to the test, like Mirella Freni and I were at the start of our careers. We also had good qualities, but we weren't exceptional. We were fortunate enough to have a broad range, though, so all we had to do was polish it. I had to struggle, sharpen my wits, perfect my technique, and sing operas I never would have dreamed of doing, but all that helped me to strengthen my voice. At one point, I was forced to go to Glyndebourne, since I was a Mozart fanatic. This was early in 1964, but I realised I had to do it right away, without wasting time. I had to learn to sing softly. Anyone who has a voice can sing loudly. It was hard."

This reminded me of something I had read: "In your autobiography, Joan Ingpen related: 'Glyndebourne's approach to opera is the opposite end of the spectrum from the provincial Italian school that Luciano grew up in. And Mozart was a departure from his usual repertoire. It was funny watching them coach him in Mozart, but they are terribly good and very serious - which Luciano was quick to appreciate - and when Jani Strasser was in charge of musical preparation there, Glyndebourne was a marvellous place to polish vocal technique. Jani had a big influence on Luciano. This was an important step in Pavarotti's musical development'."

"Were your Glyndebourne days really that difficult?"

"Extremely! Ms Ingpen was right to say that it was a special place: I learned there that singing softly is much much harder than singing loud. At that point I still hadn't fully grasped the problem, and I thought that singing softly meant pushing less. Instead it's something else entirely, which is hard to put into words."

I added, "So your job, your art, is arduous from beginning to end."

"Exactly. It takes will power and humility, which are both rare. That's why so many gorgeous voices, with all the assets God can give, appear and then disappear."

"Is there a lack of good teachers? Is this where you got the idea for the international competition for young singers?"

Pavarotti replied: "That's one of the many reasons. On the twentieth anniversary of my Philadelphia début, I was asked what kind of a tribute I wanted. I answered, 'If you really must give me a tribute, why not start a competition in my name and in Philadelphia? The winners could then sing with me'."

I added: "You have preliminaries all over the world, and the final competition in Philadelphia. Are there hard decisions? Does Pavarotti make the selections?"

"It's hard for them and for me. This year I heard one thousand five hundred singers and there are only forty finalists. Before making our decisions we heard them at least five times. Add it all up."

I pose a difficult question: "Who is Luciano Pavarotti?"

"I couldn't tell you."

"Do you still try to understand, or have you given up?"

"Maybe I don't care. If I had to understand who I am, maybe I wouldn't be myself any more."

"Luciano, there are many great conductors in America. One of them, Kurt Herbert Adler of the San Francisco Opera, who is a good friend of yours and whom you vacation with, once asked you to sing a piece from *Aïda* in concert. You answered, 'I'll have to think about it.' He replied: 'Don't even try it. Everyone knows that tenors have no brains'."

Pavarotti replies, "He was just joking."

"But you've proven you have a brain, in addition to your voice. I've even heard that you're a smart administrator."

"No, I'm a disaster as an administrator, but my wife is great. Try to understand me. I think I'm a poet, and poets are always losing money. In the past I even made certain investments."

"Could you explain?"

"I made investments that made no sense, that I hadn't gone looking for, but that came to me along with all the other things life proposes. Well, all those investments were failures."

"In what sense?"

"In the sense that I didn't make any money, and I might have lost some."

"At a certain point you became a citizen of Monaco. Why?"

"To be honest with you, the Tortora case convinced me to do this.

151

(Translator's note: Enzo Tortora was a popular television host, imprisoned in the 1980s on suspicion of involvement in drug trafficking, and released when the allegations were proven unfounded.)

"There was such a backlash against him that I was frightened, and since . . . I want to use the right words here, because it's a delicate subject. I live in Italy for one or two months a year, and work here maybe twenty days a year. A singer, any singer, who leads this kind of life is not required to maintain residence in Italy, and can choose to reside wherever he or she wishes. I had never given this much thought, until the Tortora case exploded. Then I told myself: I'd better get out of here, because if they want to have a good time scapegoating a celebrity, only because he is a celebrity, that's not right. And so I left, but only in the fiscal sense. I could never really leave - I love living in Modena too much, when I can. Since then I've been more free to do what I want, especially for my city. Now I can do more than before, because I don't have to worry about being misunderstood."

I ask Pavarotti for clarification: "Isn't your Monaco residence also a way of avoiding paying taxes twice? In the United States and in many other countries taxes are deducted the moment you are paid."

"Taxes were only a secondary concern. At year's end there's very little difference. I could have come to an agreement with the Italian Treasury."

"Luciano, your father was a baker. What does bread mean to you?"

"Bread is our daily bread. Bread is essential. It's something you must never throw away. Jesus Christ bent down to pick it up."

"Is friendship important for a world traveller like yourself?"

"It's indispensable. I have to see my friends and telephone them long distance."

"Umberto Boeri, one of your childhood friends, said 'Being Pavarotti's friend is exciting.' Why?"

"Ask him."

"Who was Umberto Boeri in your youth?"

"A close friend. He studied medicine, and after graduating from the University of Modena he went to the United States, studied English, went to medical school, and became a paediatrician. He's one of the nicest people I know. We're friends because he, like me, has will power."

"Another friend of yours, who used to sing with you, is in the chorus of the Maggio Musicale Fiorentino."

"You must mean Bindo Guerrini, another friend I can always count on."

"You have had an amazing, triumphant, brilliant career, while he remained a singer in the chorus. How do you feel about that?"

"It's hard to say. I don't want to judge. I would say that I yearned for something that Guerrini may have wanted less. I also got my start earlier: I was nineteen, and he was already twenty-six."

"What remains between two friends who sing together but whose careers go in such different directions? Does this affect your friendship?"

"Not at all. My friendship with Bindo has always been the same."

"Do you feel a special affection toward him, the way you might feel toward someone who has had less from life?"

"Let's be clear about what you mean by 'less'. I am Bindo's friend for what he is, not for what he sings. He may even be happier, in the chorus, than yours truly . . . I'll have to ask him some day."

"Your wife Adua."

"My woman, my destiny, my strength. This isn't just rhetoric. Without her I would never have attained the goals I dreamed of. She also leads a hard life. When she's not with me she's always at her desk or on the phone. The other day she had to go to an office. When she saw the receptionist, rather than say *Buongiorno*, she said *Pronto*, is Mr So-and-so there, as if she were talking on the telephone."

"How do you get along with your daughters?"

"Like a brother. For me they're like sisters, and sometimes like mothers."

"Is it true they spoil you?"

"Hardly! The opposite is true. They treat me 'bad', but that's OK."

"Lorenza was born in 1962, Cristina in 1964, and Giuliana in 1967. Then you said 'stop,' before having any sons."

"Not really. I didn't say stop. The man isn't the one to have babies; the woman is, so I think my wife is the one who decided not to have any more. She had every right to make that decision, and three is the perfect number for children, too."

"In a television interview for *Odeon*, you told me that you worship women. You were singing the part of Nemorino in *L'Elisir d'Amore*, The Elixir of Love. Nemorino is a character who loses his head and becomes a babbling idiot for love. What is love for you?"

"This is why I love the character Nemorino. However, let me hasten to add that worshipping women doesn't mean loving all of them. But there's no doubt in my mind that after health, nothing is more important than love. There is the love for a woman, for your children, for your parents, for your sister, for your friends, and for your neighbour, which I feel in a particularly strong way. It is very, very important, and sometimes it makes me crazy."

"Are you faithful to your wife?"

"I'm so faithful I must be boring."

"In that same interview you told me that when a man falls in love he becomes a little silly."

"No doubt about it. Because he loses all his strength. Maybe the same thing happens to women, but a woman is much more likely to fall in love with love itself. Women are different, and inside them is the mystery and the gift of life. They can experience love in a different way, and know a deeper love, but they will never deny themselves to the point of becoming idiotic. They also know how to suffer better, and with greater dignity."

"In the early years of your career they called you 'Passion Flower'."

"What did they call me?"

"Passion Flower."

"I don't remember."

"Luciano, they say that you flirted with all the women when you went to Glyndebourne to improve your Mozart."

"That's not true. It's a joke, and in very bad taste."

"But it's in your autobiography."

Pavarotti gets a little irritated, and starts looking through the book.

I hint, "On page 80."

In the meantime Pavarotti thinks out loud: "I don't think they said I flirted with all the girls. I do enjoy spending time with a woman more than with a man, but that's a different matter. Partly because I grew up surrounded by women, and it's easier for me to talk to them. I don't think it's written that way. Read it properly, please."

Pavarotti finds the right page. He reads aloud: "Luciano's eye for all the pretty girls around the opera house earned him the nickname 'Passion Flower'."

"Well, Luciano, what are we to make of this? Adua was in Modena anxiously waiting for you."

"We shall say exactly what is written in the book. Having an eye for does not mean flirting or dating. It means to have an eye for, and that's that. Adua did not deserve the slightest transgression."

Pavarotti is in great shape. He has lost weight, is rejuvenated, and satisfied.

"Let's talk about your diet for a minute. What was your experience like with Dr Andrea Strata, the chairman of Nutrition and Diet at the University of Parma, and director of the 'Health Project' at the baths of Tabiano di Salsomaggiore?"

"We followed a diet I had already followed in 1975 with Mrs Franca Corfini. This diet is based on calories, the total abstention from certain substances and foods, like sugar and alcohol. Fats are taken only in the right amount. For me the experience was OK because you eat well. Very well. It's not so much a diet, as a lesson about food."

The interview ends in the kitchen. For Pavarotti, an evening at home at last. "Tonight I'm going to cook the spaghetti," he says. He fills the kettle with water, and prepares a sauce according to Dr Strata's instructions. The napkin he's wearing around his neck reminds me of the huge handkerchief he holds in concerts.

"Why do you carry that huge handkerchief?"

"When I did my first concert I didn't know where to put my hands, so I decided to hold them steady with this handkerchief. In the first half of the concert I almost tore it to shreds; by the second half my hands were already more relaxed, and I was moving them more loosely. I used it again, and then it turned into a kind of lucky charm."

"Do you ever get tired of being who you are?"

"If I knew who I was, I might, or I might not. I get along well with myself because I grew up very slowly, and not in a single day. I'm still the same person I used to be. But now there is this enormous responsibility, the enormous joy over my career that makes so many people love me. There have been no great changes in me otherwise."

"Once you said that Modena didn't encourage you at all. How is your relationship to the city and its inhabitants today?"

"Fantastic, marvellous, serene. I don't need them any more, and they don't need me. We have an open relationship. And the Teatro Comunale has changed management."

The spaghetti might get overcooked. That would not sit well with Pavarotti, who's finally home.

At the door I ask him, "What does Modena mean to you?"

He replies, "Whatever it means to you."

"In other words, a great deal, almost everything."

"Exactly."

WHISTLE WHILE YOU
WORK

The first time I met the great conductor Herbert von Karajan was in the Okura Hotel in Tokyo. Until then I had only seen him in pictures and on television. I imagined him to be tall, imposing and dictatorial. I got into the elevator and suddenly there he was: tiny, fragile, with neatly-combed white hair.

Herbert von Karajan once said that every time he worked with Pavarotti "it was a party", and in the letter he sent to Modena for the celebration of Pavarotti's twenty-fifth year of singing, he wrote: "*Lieber Luciano, Ich freue Mich, dass Sie unter Meiner Leitung zum ersten Mal La Bohème an der Scala sangen.*" (Dear Luciano, I am happy that the first time you sang *La Bohème* at La Scala it was under my direction.)

It was an important day for Pavarotti when he garnered top marks from the great Austrian conductor, who would remember Luciano's performance in Verdi's *Requiem* as: *Eindrucksvolles*, deeply impressive.

Maestro Leone Magiera considers the focal point of Pavarotti's career, aside from his partnering with Sutherland and his Mozart training, to have been his meeting with von Karajan, who immediately sensed his great talent, and conducted him in his La Scala début in *La Bohème*.

Gustav Kuhn, a student of Herbert von Karajan lives in Erl, in the Tyrolean Alps. He was born in Salzburg: "a city famous for three reasons - because Mozart, von Karajan, and Niki Lauda were born there."

I ask, "Please tell me your immediate reaction to the triumph of the Bologna performances of *Ballo in Maschera*, which you conducted, Maestro."

"I am convinced that Pavarotti represents a culture that unfortunately is fading. By this I mean a musical culture, a style of performing, the ability to assimilate the spirit of a score, the fidelity to the great composers' image of a character."

"What did you learn about Pavarotti?"

"That he doesn't just sing for himself, but for the whole ensemble. He expresses his ideas and wants to realise them in order to raise everybody to a higher level."

"They say that Pavarotti is a great voice, but above all a great professional."

"It's true. He knows when he has to use all his energies, and when he can reserve them. He is punctual and disciplined. Many singers, when asked to appear for rehearsals at 10:30, will come to the theatre asking everyone to wait because they don't feel ready, and then go on stage half an hour later. Pavarotti is different, and perhaps unique. For him 10:30 means 10:30, not a minute more or a minute less. Pavarotti goes on stage at the scheduled time, and sings in full form. Naturally when he is there no one dares to complain, or play for time. Pavarotti teaches that there is a discipline to respect. With him a rehearsal always begins with top concentration."

"They say that you are very demanding. You're a little over forty, yet already you're known all over the world for your punctuality."

"Some people think I'm excessive in demanding such punctuality and discipline, but Pavarotti understood me. It was important to me to have his approval. He said, 'Bravo, that's the way to work'. With Luciano, thanks to his punctuality, I was always able to let the orchestra go half an hour early because we worked with the maximum concentration. With Pavarotti you go to the heart of problems and solve them quickly. He creates an almost magical relationship, and his presence is fundamental. When only the orchestra was busy, he would sit in the fourteenth row and follow our rehearsals for hours. I never saw a singer of his level so careful, so involved in following the execution of a score from note to note."

"Your collaboration with him produced great results."

"We were thinking together, like mediums. I instantly understood what he was thinking. I learned a great deal from Pavarotti, and I hadn't improved my own professionalism so much in so little time since studying with von Karajan."

"So it's true that Pavarotti gives good advice to conductors?"

"Definitely. He also knows how to propose things at just the right moment and in just the right way. He never says 'I need this,' but rather suggests, 'I understand, but what I would try is . . .'; or 'Why don't we try this? I'd be curious to see how it works'. I also studied philosophy and psychology, and to me it was important to discover this side of Pavarotti's artistic personality. He lives and sings intelligently, his goal is perfection; he sings with his heart, but mainly with his head."

"Would you describe your first meeting with Pavarotti?"

"It was in the foyer of the Teatro Comunale of Bologna. He had just arrived from the United States, and was a little tired from jet lag. He immediately told me: 'Tomorrow we can have two rehearsals, and I definitely won't be able to sing for the last three hours, but the day after tomorrow I'll be at your complete disposal'."

"Is Pavarotti, almost a German . . .?"

"A German as far as discipline goes, but an Italian at heart."

"Did you have any problems living side by side for a month?"

"Never. We worked seriously and cheerfully. We allowed ourselves a few dinners with the orchestra. We also teased each other about our bellies. He had lost over seventy pounds. When we met he patted my stomach, joking 'You don't like to eat'. He told me he wants to lose even more weight. Maybe we'll go to Tabiano together."

"Before conducting him in *Ballo* had you ever heard Pavarotti?"

"Yes, in a concert in Salzburg fifteen years ago. I was immediately amazed by him. He started to sing, and you could see that he was tense. Herbert von Karajan and his wife were in the audience, as were Mirella Freni, many critics, and musicians. Then a little at a time he loosened up and the concert ended with the entire audience on its feet. There was half an hour of applause, and no one wanted to go home."

I commented, "Some people say that Pavarotti has the world's most fascinating voice."

"A reporter asked the ninety-year-old Arthur Rubinstein, 'Why do you think the public is so fascinated by you?' He answered: 'Maybe there are a thousand pianists out there who are better than I am, but only two or three put their whole heart, all their feelings, into the music'. I think that Pavarotti is a little like Rubinstein. The beauty of his voice is unquestionable, his intensity draws you in, but every moment of Pavarotti's interpretation is full of all the emotions a man has inside. This is why the public identifies with him. Technique is fundamental, but if you don't have those feelings inside you . . . I have also directed opera, and I always tell the singers, 'Put everything you have into it, enter into the character'."

"Pavarotti at fifty-three still has a splendid voice, and is getting even better."

"Because he sings the right repertory in the right way."

"Maestro Kuhn, in your opinion a great conductor . . ."

He bursts out laughing, "Pavarotti is a great conductor."

"No one has said this yet. Pavarotti the director, Pavarotti the singer, Pavarotti Pavarottissimo, and now conductor!"

"I'm serious. During one of the last rehearsals of *Ballo*, at the beginning of the third act, when the tenor is not on stage, Pavarotti got up from his seat in the fourteenth row, came up beside me, and slipped the baton out of my hand. Then he started to conduct. The musicians just kept on playing as if nothing had changed, and then there was a great burst of applause."

"Would you do a serious, professional analysis of this exploit?"

"Pavarotti could really be a great conductor. As we say in the field, he has a beautiful arm."

"In your opinion, who is Pavarotti?"

"After von Karajan, he is the man who has taught me the most. *Ballo in Maschera* was a continued success, and got better every time we performed it. I don't particularly like doing encores, but I had to adapt to them because the enthusiasm was overwhelming. After fifteen minutes of applause, Luciano thought that I wouldn't allow an encore, and was getting ready to continue the opera. But I stopped him, made a signal to the orchestra, and gave in to the public. Luciano kept his control for two measures, and then started to laugh. The audience was beside itself, howling with laughter. After an avalanche of applause, we tuned up, and gave the real encore."

Gustav Kuhn's father was an editor, and Gustav began studying music when he was four, conducting his first concert at nineteen. I asked him if he really thought he could be von Karajan's heir, and he ruled out that possibility. "Anyone who tried to imitate him would be making a mistake. The times have changed."

"But many critics are right to say there are two kinds of conductors: Karajan, and the others."

I asked Kuhn why there was such a thinning in the ranks of the great singers.

He replied: "There's too much of a rush to make it, too much immaturity, and too little time to study. Nowadays, many singers burn out quickly. They're like beautiful plants that suddenly wither. A singer should think about building his or her career in the right doses, and cultivating the beauty and intensity of the voice. Not many singers pace themselves as carefully as Luciano: he had patience and intelligence. Not many people realise how many times he has refused a role because it wasn't right for him, or the hundreds of times he said no because he wasn't sure he could give his best in an interpretation. Pavarotti knows that singing is a terribly serious business. One fact explains his personality very well. When he sings in Bologna, he never goes home (though Modena is only twenty-seven kilometres away), not even on his day off. He stays in the hotel, and goes for quick walks. He avoids distractions, even if not being able to see his parents, wife and daughters weighs on him. He stays in Bologna as if he were in New York. After the first act of *Ballo* when I brought a small gift to him on stage, he said, 'I have nothing to give you, because I didn't leave the hotel yesterday or today: the night before an opening, tenors have to stay in bed'. He brought me a present the next day."

"What did he give you?"

"It's a secret."

"Are you superstitious too?"

"What does superstitious mean?"

In *La Repubblica*, Fabrizio Festa confirmed that Gustav Kuhn had found a great collaborator in Pavarotti. Kuhn told him: "Pavarotti believes, as did von Karajan, that music depends on millimetres, on the small percentages, and not on the big numbers. An artist has to have ninety-five per cent profession, three per cent instinct, and the remaining two per cent distinguishes the great from the mediocre, and even from the bad. It's a question of millimetres: it's not easy to find the right balance between my sensibility, born and bred in a Middle European repertory, and the music of Verdi, which is completely immersed in Italian culture. That's why Pavarotti was so valuable. He sat in the auditorium listening and trying to understand my intentions, doing much more than he had to. At a certain point, when I told him that I didn't want to lose my identity, he smiled and said, 'We're not doing a German opera'."

FROM LUCIO DALLA
TO MINA

Why does Pavarotti sing folk songs and pop tunes? Why do some people complain that it's a sacrilege? And why does he have so much fun playing the field: from the solemn opera of *Aïda* to a popular Modenese ballad, from Riccardo in *Un Ballo in Maschera* to a torch song, from Neapolitan folk songs to . . .? What will Pavarotti do tomorrow? Maybe he won't make any more movies, since his experience with *Yes, Giorgio* was hardly memorable ("But I had a good time"), but maybe he will direct another opera, even if after *La Favorita* he said, "I wanted to try the experience, I am happy with it, I'll stop here."

But did he have to try light music, too? "A voice that soars in the great ensembles, as if he were drawing the chorus into his arias," is what *Time* magazine said. But did he have to venture into the area where pop singers Claudio Villa and Domenico Modugno had been so popular?

Giorgio Corzolani of the *Resto del Carlino* once suggested, "Isn't there the risk that some people will talk of betrayal?" Pavarotti replied at the top of his lungs: "What betrayal? I make records filled with good music, and good music is above distinctions of genre and style." Beniamino Gigli and Tito Schipa felt the same way.

Recently Stella Pende of *L'Europeo* asked Pavarotti: "You've also sung popular songs, which some people considered a concession to the more profitable field of light music." His answer was very specific: "For me music is all one thing. It's neither heavy nor light. For that matter, a song like 'Lolita' was written for Caruso, while 'Mamma' was written for Gigli and 'Vivere' for Schipa. Is my singing 'Caruso' by Lucio Dalla a concession? Then fine, I consider it a masterpiece, and I'm happy I sang it." He also confided to his interviewer that one of his dreams was to sing with Mina, "Wherever and whenever she wants; I really admire her."

Daniel Rubboli had some thoughts about Pavarotti's forays into light music when the latest album by Luciano Pavarotti topped the international charts: "Big Luciano, alias the most popular and top-grossing tenor in the world (estimates of his worth vary between fifty and one hundred million dollars), the only tenor since Gigli who has succeeded in sitting on Caruso's throne, has routed the competition once again, putting his name, voice, and style on the album *Volare*, which he recorded with Henry Mancini, the composer of numerous film soundtracks and winner of four Academy Awards."

Pavarotti sold millions of copies of the albums *Mamma* and *Passione*, but he wanted to pay homage to Domenico Modugno with *Volare*. He told Rubboli: "Flying is my dream, and it was also Modugno's dream. Did you ever dream of flying? Of feeling suspended in mid-air? I sang the beginning and end of the song in a very special way, coming up with my interpretation during the recording, instinctively, right there on the spot, to show that this is my dream, our dream, everybody's dream. But maybe I won't sing it that way anymore: with Domenico there, the atmosphere was very special, almost magical." On the same album, Pavarotti also paid homage to Mario del Monaco by singing 'Un Amore Così Grande', and to the city of Modena with 'Fra tanta gente', a song he wrote himself in collaboration with a jazz pianist from Modena, Pippo Casarini.

In late 1988, after recording Lucio Dalla's 'Caruso' (the theme song for Sophia Loren's made-for-television movie *Mamma Lucia*), Pavarotti realised that he had found the right partner for the field of light music, to follow up the record-breaking sales of his albums of operatic duets with Mirella Freni, Joan Sutherland and Katia Ricciarelli. After word of this got out, Vittorio Spiga of the *Resto del Carlino* interviewed an emotional Lucio Dalla, who was beginning to worry about this unusual collaboration. Dalla confirmed: "It was Pavarotti's idea. Evidently he enjoyed singing my 'Caruso'. For my part, I have to confess that I was amazed at the great Luciano's flexibility, and at his willingness to be a pop singer, which of course is in the tradition of the most famous tenors. A tenor doesn't have to be tied to his operatic essence, no matter how great the results. Pavarotti can sing anything."

Dalla then confessed that he had thought about collaborating with Pavarotti after 'Caruso', but that he hadn't dared propose it: "I didn't think he would trust me with such an important job." When Spiga asked him how their collaboration began, he explained: "It all started with the feeling established between Pavarotti and I when he recorded 'Caruso'. I was paralysed by his bravura and by his versatility, and didn't know what to say. There I was with the greatest tenor in the world, who has an incredible sense of rhythm, and an exceptional ability to leave behind the strictures of his own musical universe. When he started to broach the idea, I knew it would represent a fantastic opportunity to write something for Pavarotti."

Spiga asked, "Where do you think Pavarotti's sense of rhythm comes from?"

Dalla replied: "It's a gift, but it also comes from his Emilian origins. He was born in a region with a greater musical heritage than most others. In addition, Pavarotti is full of curiosity. He's interested in other areas of music and of the performing arts. He is a good manager, very cultured, and has started directing. This is typical of people from Emilia-Romagna - they're never satisfied, and are always thinking of the future."

"Will Pavarotti's record include only your songs?"

"No. It might not include any of my songs. I'm not sure I'll be able to write anything important enough for a great tenor like Luciano. I am producing the album, and arranging it with Malavasi, who's a wonderful musician. Pavarotti and I are choosing the songs together. There'll be one by Guida, one by Bernstein, and one by Francesco Guccini. There are many people working for him. Obviously I'd love to put in some of my own work as well."

"Did Pavarotti ask you to?"

"Yes, we made some plans, but they're still tentative. I'm always a little awkward even when I'm making one of my own albums, so you can imagine how it is with a big-shot like Pavarotti."

"He could sing one of your old hits."

"I'd like to give him something new, but an old song would be OK too. Pavarotti proposed lending his voice to 'Lucio dove vai?' which I wrote twenty years ago. He told me he enjoys it. Maybe he identifies with the name. At any rate, Pavarotti knows full well what's best for him. He's so close to today's musical feeling that it almost makes me jealous. He's hardly unprepared."

Pavarotti is certainly not unprepared, but at the same time he is trying not to lose whatever little personal space he has left. In the summer of 1988, he turned down a two-hundred million lira engagement offered by a company that wanted him as the star among stars for a special celebration. But they had to do without him. He refused to interrupt his vacation in Pesaro, where he built a photographer-proof villa (after some pàparazzi caught him in a bathing suit, sporting all those extra pounds he would later lose). But Pavarotti has very specific ideas about pop songs, and is very hard on people who try to send him cautionary messages: "Certain songs are a part of history, sung by millions of people. You can't just dismiss them with the label 'pop tunes'."

Lucio Dalla confirms this. "We are doing songs that are beautiful only if people use them, exchange them, and keep them in their hearts. My albums are full of characters who came to me on their own, and gave shape to my imagination. I tell true stories; in another time I would have been a troubadour, or a chronicler."

In *La Repubblica*, Claudia Casini wrote: "For a tenor there is a big difference between opera and songs, and between the theatre and a concert. On stage, a singer is always encumbered by his or her costume. In a song, everything is different: the tenor is naked, with no make-up, and without a character to hide behind. He has to construct a world of feelings and images, and express the emotions they convey through words and music. High notes are useless, or they're only good for topping off an interpretation that has been constructed in every detail. In a certain sense, songs are a kind of ultimate test for a tenor, partly because the words and music are often better than in opera. There's a great repertory of songs, especially from the second half of the nineteenth century to the early twentieth century. Will Pavarotti and Dalla succeed in restoring the gentle melancholy of past songs to us?"

Rodolfo Celletti, who holds Luciano in great esteem, has his doubts. In his last book, *Opera In Disco*, he wrote: "Pavarotti is charming, intelligent and clever. Of today's acclaimed tenors, he has by far the best form. One month ago he sang a splendid *Ballo In Maschera* in Bologna, with a youthful voice. It's a shame that now he has been sidetracked onto the repertory of Schipa, Tagliavini and Gigli. They sang those songs much better. You need preparation for songs, too. Either Pavarotti doesn't realise this, or he's pretending that he doesn't."

BRAVURA AND
HUMILITY

"When I was with Giulia I felt like I was in heaven."
If you want to understand something more about
Luciano Pavarotti, you must invoke the magic,
mythic name of his grandmother Giulia. "She
understood me and always protected me. She was very intelligent, and very philosophical in her way." This is how Pavarotti
explained the central motif of a happy childhood in his autobiography. He built a vacation home in Pesaro, and dedicated it
to her: 'Villa Giulia'. He explains: "She rarely restrained or disciplined me but treated me like a little wild animal, a precious
animal, one with a soul."

He's been called "the king of tenors", and in the United States
they wish they could book him solid for the whole year, from
coast to coast. Whenever he sings at the Metropolitan Opera the
performance is sold out months in advance. To cope with the
pressure, Luciano often takes refuge in his memories. Giulia's
name is always with him. One of his daughters is named
Giuliana. Pavarotti says that memory is a fundamental part of
life. Inner balance counts, too.

Ennio Cavalli interviewed him at Villa Giulia, and was

amazed at the pace of his work: "He is able to take on the most diverse engagements, in the most varied places and conditions: operas, solo recitals, benefit concerts, recording sessions and live broadcasts. You also have to add aeroplane flights, rigid diets, official dinners, press conferences, rest on command, and naturally, constant study." Luciano Pavarotti loves humble things like homemade pasta, but he also likes to take the time to ponder on the great existential questions too. He didn't shove other people aside to make it, for as he told Cavalli, "What matters in life is knowing how to do your part with bravura and humility."

George Cehanosky, a former baritone who was the glory of the Met, said he has, "Vigour, enthusiasm, tenderness, sweetness, style and sincerity in his singing, like we haven't seen in fifty years. Pavarotti is a complete singer; he has all these qualities, but he uses his head. I don't see him in the part of Satan."

It's been said that Pavarotti is Caruso's heir. In his autobiography Pavarotti expressed his thoughts on the Neapolitan tenor at length: "As for Caruso, there are no comparisons. With all due respect, I do not agree with Maestro von Karajan's remarkable comment that my voice is greater. To me, Caruso is rightly the tenor against whom all the rest of us are measured. I do not say this so much for his voice, which was indeed very beautiful and too distinctive for comparisons. He started as a baritone and always had the brown colour of a deeper voice. I say this because, with his incredible phrasing and musical instincts, he came closer than any of us to the music he sang. There will never be another like him.

"I don't know what Caruso's secret was and I don't want to know. Everyone must find his own secret. Tenors who try to imitate Caruso usually lose their voices. It is all but impossible to sing the way someone else sang. And you cannot forget the personality, either. A voice expresses the composer's music, to be sure, but it also expresses the personality of the singer. To set out after another's voice is a profound mistake. So while I am naturally flattered by comparisons with Caruso, they also worry me. I hope to achieve something special in my own way, not his. We are two different tenors."

One of the great music critics, Mario Pasi of the *Corriere della Sera*, said: "Who is Pavarotti? The good hero." I asked Pasi, who has followed every step of Pavarotti's career, for a quick sketch of the celebrity and of the man who was "enthralled" by the sound of the organ as a child. "Mr Pasi, some people maintain that Pavarotti is the last great tenor. Should we believe this, or is it just an attempt to enhance his legend?"

Pasi replies, "Despite all my love for Pavarotti, I would be very sorry if he had no heirs. There will be other good or great tenors, but not right away. It's always dangerous to create legends."

"Professor Pasi, someone once tried to convince Pavarotti to play the part of Caruso in a film. He refused, saying it would show a lack of respect towards him. What is the difference between Caruso and Pavarotti? Was he right to turn the part down?"

Pasi replied: "Comparisons are risky. Enrico Caruso was certainly the greatest tenor of his day. I wish I could have heard him sing live. Pavarotti has more style and better phrasing, as our own day and age demand. He was right to turn down the part of Caruso in the film because he's a smart man, and he realises that he's too well known to pass himself off as someone else."

I ask: "In his early days Pavarotti studied Mozart at length. Did he need to do this?"

"Definitely. Mozart is a master of style and intelligence. He helps you realise how great music really is."

"Pavarotti has been particularly attentive to his diction. Is it true that diction is his distinctive trait?"

"Today a singer has to have good diction. Pavarotti has no rivals in this area."

"Who is more congenial to Pavarotti: Bellini, Donizetti or Verdi?"

"That's easy: all three. Then he makes his own choices from the repertoire of each."

"Which character is best suited to his voice?"

"The good hero, as in *Ballo in Maschera* or *La Bohème*. But the list is much longer."

"Pavarotti decided to direct an opera. After the performance, he said, 'I'll never do this again'. What did you think of his attempt?"

"His production of *La Favorita* in Venice was a diversion for him. I agree that it was an isolated instance. In the future, we'll see."

"Pavarotti still doesn't know whether he'll do the title role in Verdi's *Otello*, but lately he's hinted on several occasions that he will do it. What kind of Otello can we expect from him?"

"For the time being I don't think he will do *Otello*. If he does decide to sing it in the near future, his interpretation could be a big surprise, because he'll give the character, the Moor of Venice, a spark that other singers have failed to strike."

I comment: "Pavarotti gave a wonderful interpretation of the Duke of Mantua in *Rigoletto*, but he claims his favourite opera is *Ballo in Maschera*. Initially he was more cautious about it, though, because he was worried that the vocal range was wrong for him. His début was in *La Bohème*, and he was a perfect Rodolfo. How do you explain these shifts?"

"Pavarotti has the right to choose, to understand year in and year out which roles are best for him, and which are best for us."

I ask, "What kind of tenor is he?"

Pasi replies: "He is a lyric tenor who can sing either light or dramatic repertoire."

"Is he an instinctive or a rational singer?"

"He's a very rational singer, but without repressing his instincts."

I ask: "He has never taken the easy way, but he has refused to sing operas that he didn't think were right for him. He knows how to take care of himself, and claims that after certain operas or after concerts his voice needs a long period of rest. Why do people believe the myth of his total human openness?"

Pasi replies: "Managing your voice well is praiseworthy. Pavarotti has lasted longer than many other singers who played themselves out quickly. His humanity has little to do with his singing; it's a question of character. He's charming, and moreover he's rational. He's a rationalist."

"What about Pavarotti and songs. Some people think Pavarotti shouldn't have given in so easily. Do you agree?"

"All the tenors did it, including Caruso. The art song is respectable; the pop song less so. I think Pavarotti showed good judgement in this. Personally I think 'Mamma' was quite good, 'Volare' not as good."

"Pavarotti's voice has changed since his début in Reggio Emilia. What were the fundamental phases of his career?"

"It would be tragic if a tenor didn't improve after his début. Pavarotti polished his natural talents through study and will power. He went from being the king of the high C's to the king of expression. His voice is a delight to the ear, which explains everything."

I ask: "Is it true that Pavarotti goes beyond the libretto? Why does he claim that a singer can help improve an intuition that an author did not make completely explicit?"

"A composer dreams that singers will understand what he wanted in addition to the notes. The singer can and must 'enter into that dream' - at his or her own risk. The score is not a simple sequence of black dots, lines, and technical signs. Art is nurtured by the translation of those signs, which come to life in the individual expression of the person reading them. I wouldn't say the singer 'improves', but rather gets closer to the truth of the creative act."

"Who is the true Pavarotti?"

"Pavarotti is very attached to his region and to his people, but he is also very American. Who is the true Pavarotti? If we multiply his weight by a thousand, we might get the right answer."

"There has always been a love-hate relationship between Pavarotti and La Scala. He claims that he always reserves a month for La Scala, and they never call him. How did this misunderstanding come about?"

"With La Scala there are no misunderstandings, only momentary difficulties. Working at La Scala is more complicated than at the Met, where there is less artistic discipline and the schedule is more reliable."

"Dame Joan Sutherland said that Luciano is the master of his career. Is this true?"

"The opposite would be strange."

"In your opinion, Pasi, how would you sum up Luciano Pavarotti?"

"A lyric artist, and a champion of humanity."

JUDGEMENT DAY

My circumnavigation of Pavarotti will now come to a close with three *loggionisti* from Parma. The *loggionisti*, regular audience members in the galleries of the Italian opera houses, are the self-proclaimed guardians of opera. Usually veterans of several decades of theatre-going, the success or resounding failure of a performance can depend entirely on their whims. The *loggionisti* of La Scala and the Parma Reggio are particularly notorious for their abilty to bring down a performance with their whistles and boos. Do they have ferocious faces or cannibal mouths? Hardly. Representing the group of two hundred are a mild-mannered gentleman, a polite business consultant, and a calm if somewhat fussy pensioner, named Dr Gianalessandro Isi. But all three of them have unforgettable eyes which scrutinise you warily before finally conceding a glimmer of cordiality. They are the custodians of a sacred tradition, and wish to defend their reputation as implacable judges. They say: "If we give in it's over. Today, with automatic applause, always and everywhere, we miss whistling. What a beautiful thing it is to boo, or even give raspberries, as they once did to a tenor in the Regio Theatre, which we consider a temple . . . no, an altar."

I interrupt, "An altar on which you sacrifice your victims, if you can."

"Let's not exaggerate. We give an honest opinion, defend the art of *bel canto*, beautiful singing, the style natural to operas by Bellini, Donizetti, Rossini and Verdi. We try at all costs to prevent the lowering of the standards of pure and even singing of the solo melody line. We're ready to applaud, but booing can be very valuable. It can be worth more than a hundred voice lessons, more than any number of vocalisations; it can straighten out an absent-minded young singer, and make him or her think about the need for hard work. Because singing is an extremely hard career. Do you want us to talk about Pavarotti? Well he became Pavarotti by working his way up. He was a real bohemian before singing about it on stage. Today's singers should learn from him."

"Dr Isi, who is Pavarotti?"

He looks at me askance, and realises that he is about to make an important concession. "We could say that Pavarotti . . . is one of the greatest *bel canto* singers of the past fifty years." If Luciano were here he might breathe a sigh of relief; he has conquered the United States, collected triumphs the world over, but he has never sung an entire opera in Parma. The *loggionisti* have had to travel to make up their minds about him, so he still has an important appointment. Who cares about the Met, La Scala, or the Royal Opera House, Covent Garden? If he wants his final laurel, he still has to come to the Regio of Parma. The two hundred ladies and gentlemen of the former duchy of Parma, where everything seems steeped in the perfume of violets, have the right to hear Pavarotti in an opera, and not just in the two concerts he has already given there.

Here we are in the land of Verdi and Toscanini, inside a mechanism that is at once magical and iron-clad. In Parma, opera is not child's play. You first take your seat in the gallery when you're ten; for Gianalessandro Isi it was the beginning of a love story, of a wild passion, of applause, protests and subtle dissertations. "We go to the theatre well prepared, and weigh our judgements on a pharmacist's scales. It's hard for us to make a mistake. But unlike *loggionisti* of past decades, we see more performances, and are able to listen to perfect recordings. But even before applause was never for free, and protests were never gratuitous. The *loggionisti* are not merely folkloric."

The outrage of the distinguished gentlemen of Parma once came down on the head of Vittorio De Santi. In the 1950s, he was so irritated by their protests against his performance of *Otello* that he threw his sword at the audience. When the tenor Mori saw his Manrico rejected, he had to throw in the towel. But the worst fate was in store for the tenor Ruggero Bondino. With proud remorse, Ferruccio Frigieri admits, "We may have destroyed his career." The truth is that poor Bondino did all right in the end, but his appearance in *La Traviata* at the Regio was a disaster. The audience's expression of contempt was so violent that the poor tenor tried to hide backstage, but a group of musclemen dragged him back on stage to wallow in shame. Years later Frigieri admits compassionately, "He didn't really have such a bad voice, but he was tone-deaf, and sometimes he bleated." The Parma *loggionisti* express even their regrets with reservation, because according to Dr Isi, "If you lower your guard anything could happen."

But the singers have always borne the brunt of it. There was a memorable performance of *Ballo in Maschera* with the American baritone Cornell MacNeil, who had to put up with the audience's murmuring during his third-act duet with the soprano. This was followed by loud comments from the gallery such as, "You idiots, you slobs." Before the aria 'Eri tu', MacNeil threw all the props on the table into the air, hurled an inkpot at the orchestra, made an obscene gesture at the audience, and left the theatre never to return.

What happened to Antonio Annaloro was almost comic. He had to cover for Gastone Limarilli after a disastrous first act of *Andrea Chenier*, but he had the misfortune to do worse. The *loggionisti* still wanted to hear the baritone Piero Cappuccili sing his pieces, so they carried out a unique form of protest. They entered and exited the gallery, applauding if Cappuccili was on stage, and signalling by their presence or absence their total disapproval of the other singers.

A performance of *La Traviata* was saved by Renato Bruson, who garnered a storm of applause. "His fellow artists and the conductor were drowned out with boos, and if it hadn't been for the baritone, the opera would have ended after the first act," Frigieri remembers. Dr Isi adds nostalgically, "Today we've gotten too good. We have performances that deserve neither huge applause nor boos. Everything is so plain and sad."

But they resist, as do other groups that have formed spontaneously, and turned into factions. There is 'Parma lirica', 'Grotta Mafalda' (which takes its name from the sandwich bar where it was founded), 'Club dei 27' (an off-shoot of 'Grotta Mafalda') and 'la Corale Verdi' (founded in 1905). A dispute several years ago over the quantity of Verdi's output led to the splintering off of 'Grotta Mafalda'. Did Verdi write twenty-seven operas or twenty-nine? The Verdi Institute was unable to settle the disagreement, because neither faction was willing to give in. The '27' left the parent organisation slamming the door, claiming that the operas *Jerusalem* and *Aroldo* were revisions of previous works (*I Lombardi alla prima crociata* and *Stiffelio*) rather than separate operas. They distanced themselves by openly telling the press and the public their code names (each member took the name of one of Verdi's '27' operas), which had been a solemn secret with the '29' members of the 'Grotta'.

Until now, I've been speaking with Isi and Frigieri at the little bar where the organisation gathers. Now that we have to "weigh" Pavarotti, they think we had better consult the president, so we go to visit the business consultant, Enrico Ghidini, at his office in central Parma, where two rooms are dedicated to Giuseppe Verdi and Maria Callas. Since Ghidini is the president, he is willing to reveal his code name. "I am *I Lombardi alla prima crociata.*" He then explains how the idea for the '27' and for the '29' originated. "Verdi is only known for two or three works. We wanted people - even those who don't go to the opera so often - to know the Maestro for his other operas, which are equally beautiful."

But we are here to talk about Luciano Pavarotti, and it's hard to pin down Ghidini and his friends, who open every season at the Regio by handing the baton to the conductor. Finally their attention shifts from Verdi to Pavarotti.

I ask: "What feeling is there between Pavarotti and Verdi?"

Ghidini answers: "Pavarotti sang a splendid *Rigoletto*, but I would have trouble calling him a Verdian tenor. He was great in *I Lombardi*, but his repertoire is much broader, and is not limited to Verdi. Certainly every time he sang one of the Maestro's operas, his performance was more than satisfactory." When you consider that this statement comes from "*Lombardi*" himself, it's no small admission. He then adds: "I adore Pavarotti, and his art is without peer. Domingo and Carreras cannot compare. Domingo is still living on past accomplishments, while Carreras is monotonous."

"But is Pavarotti still legendary?"

"I don't believe in legends, and Italy has stopped producing them. The Pavarotti legend started in the United States. They even convinced him to sing '*Fratelli d'Italia*' (the Italian national anthem) before a tennis tournament, which was hardly a great idea. I think there are many things Pavarotti should never have done, but there is a ruthless law in the Big Apple and its environs. A star always has to act like a star, make appearances, record albums and sing everything. But Pavarotti has defended himself well on the last point, and has had the courage to say no."

"Some people have criticised his incursion into pop music."

"They forget that Pavarotti is not the first tenor to go outside the operatic repertoire. When you came in I was listening to Gigli in 'Papaveri e papere'. Selections like this are dictated by the star system. Would it be blasphemous to recall that Caruso also became famous by singing Neapolitan songs? Didn't Schipa and Di Stefano do the same?"

"Mr Ghidini, looking into the future, do you think Pavarotti will be able to sing *Otello*?"

"Everyone is wondering, including me. *Otello* is a peak, an arrival point. Corelli promised he would sing it for years, and then decided not to. A tenor has to decide to sing it at the right time, and Pavarotti is on the threshold."

"Pavarotti has only sung in Parma twice."

"Yes, too little. He gave a great concert with the Verdi Chorale at the Regio, and sang Verdi's *Requiem* in the Cathedral with the orchestra and chorus of La Scala, conducted by Claudio Abbado. Our own Romano Gandolfi was the chorus master. It was triumphant, packing the Cathedral, filling the piazza, with an audio-video hook-up to the Teatro Farnese and to the Lobby."

"So Pavarotti enjoyed your full support."

"We still want to hear him in an opera."

"You've probably heard him sing in other cities."

"Yes, but the Verdian atmosphere of Parma is something else. This is the only place where a final judgement can be reached. Did you know that the Regio has the best acoustics in the world?"

"Pavarotti has also been booed."

"We were there that night at La Scala, for *Lucia di Lammermoor*. He got stuck in the final aria, 'Tu che a Dio spiegasti l'ale.' I think that's what the audience was waiting for. But Pavarotti had sung the rest of the opera superbly. The truth is that in Italy we love demolishing legends. It gives us a kind of sadistic satisfaction."

"Maybe only to you *loggionisti*, who pan singers as often as you can."

"We only pan them when it's right, or rather when we have to. We also keep things in proportion. There was another time when Pavarotti got stuck in the aria 'Spirito gentil' from *La Favorita*. But Pavarotti is an intelligent singer, and he recognises his mistakes. That time, in the mid-1960s, he was travelling back and forth between America and Italy, fighting jet lag all the way. He made his mistake, learned his lesson, and started to manage himself better. Pavarotti only entered into the hosts of the great in 1969, when he sang in Bellini's opera *I Puritani* in Bologna. He had a beautiful, high tenor voice, with perfect diction. He sang with the Parma chorus a few times, and it was breathtaking."

Frigieri comes back in, and *I Lombardi alla prima crociata* takes this opportunity to reveal Frigieri's code name: *I due Foscari*. The *Due Foscari* then elaborates on his opinion of Pavarotti. "We were among the first to realise his greatness, because from the beginning he showed how broad his repertory could be." Frigieri stops for a second, and resumes his sceptical look. "Do you mind if I dictate? I want to be specific, and I would rather not be misunderstood."

This is the way the Parma *loggionisti* are: either you accept them as they are, or they retreat behind a wall of silence. So I accept: "Go ahead, dictate away."

Frigieri begins: "Pavarotti started with Puccini, made his mark with Donizetti, and then moved on to Bellini, singing the best *Puritani* of the past fifty years. He then approached the Verdi repertoire, which may not be as congenial to his voice, with the exception of *Rigoletto*, which is his masterpiece, as is *Ballo in Maschera*."

What do the others have to add? Little or nothing. They have already reached their verdict. Now they are waiting for Pavarotti. It would be Judgement Day indeed if he came to Parma for his first *Otello*.

PAVAROTTI IN THE
POP CHARTS

In the spring of 1991, Pavarotti did sing *Otello*. He sang four performances, two in Chicago and two in New York. The opera, performed in a concert version, premièred at Orchestra Hall in Chicago, and not, as the *loggionisti* had hoped, in Parma. Pavarotti had spent the previous two years learning and perfecting the role. The performances were part of a series of farewell concerts given by the Hungarian conductor Sir Georg Solti to commemorate his 20 years with the Chicago Symphony Orchestra. Pavarotti's *Otello*, based on these performances, was recorded live by Decca.

Sadly, on the first night Pavarotti was in the throes of a very bad cold which the soprano Kiri te Kanawa, who sang the role of Desdemona, was just getting over. Solti, usually a man of vigorous health, was also suffering badly. Lesser tenors would have pulled out and no one would have blamed Pavarotti for cancelling. Later, Pavarotti spoke candidly of the dilemma he had faced. He said: "It was a question of reputation - I sang because it was my duty. As it happens, I was very pleased, because I was able to sing this opera even in such a terrible condition."

Pavarotti adds in a matter-of-fact tone, "I was not apologetic at how I sang on that first night, I was disappointed. You work for two years on a masterpiece like that, you devote yourself to it completely and then that happens. I thought my destiny deserted me. But once I heard the tape, it was not so bad." Here, Pavarotti practises what he preaches: humility and honest self-criticism. "The character was there, the vocal character, and that was very important. And I think there were some good things in New York."

Surely this is too modest an assessment for what was a remarkable highlight of Pavarotti's remarkable career! By the end of the performance on opening night, critics wrote that there was no doubt that this was a performance to tell one's grand-children about. It was a memorable interpretation and all sub-sequent performances produced enough material for a recording which could be proudly set next to the highly acclaimed recordings which already exist. Marvellous reviews from all over the world met the release of Decca's recording in the autumn of 1991. However, Pavarotti, his own greatest self-critic, lists off the other tenor and conductor partnerships who made recordings of *Otello*: "For my taste, the most close to the truth is Domingo with Levine conducting. Placido made an incredible interpretation and the orchestra was very good. But obviously there is Serafin, who made a fantastic one, Toscanini, which is the Bible of music, and von Karajan with del Monaco."

Conquering the challenge of *Otello* has had an unexpected benefit for Pavarotti. The role of *Otello* has a reputation for destroying the voices of tenors who attempt the role before they are ready. But Pavarotti said that *Otello* had given him new energy.

As Pavarotti's career moves into the new decade of the nine-ties, he is reaching ever-greater and previously undreamt of audi-ences in some of the most unexpected places. Pavarotti was one of the best selling artists of 1990. The aria 'Nessun dorma' from Puccini's opera *Turandot* was used as the BBC signature tune during the 1990 World Cup Football tournament. The television coverage of the World Cup was seen by millions and the single of

'Nessun dorma' reached number two in the UK charts while the World Cup was in progress, firmly establishing Pavarotti as a football hero and household name. Did he ever imagine as a football-crazed youth that he would some day serve his favourite sport in such a capacity?

Pavarotti went on to make chart history by becoming the first classical artist ever to reach Number One in the Pop Album Charts with the *Essential Pavarotti*. The recording stayed at number one for 10 weeks, sold more than a million copies and continues selling. Another album *Essential Pavarotti II* was released on 8 July 1991 and was equally successful. It too reached the elusive position of Number One.

Perhaps it is fitting that after having received very mixed notices for dipping into popular songs, Pavarotti answered his critics by putting opera itself into the pop charts. Now even people who would never have normally even considered listening to opera know the name of Pavarotti and possess his recordings.

But the *Essential Pavarotti* albums were not the only operatic recordings to make it to the top of the Pop Charts. The award winning, fastest and best selling classical album of all time was the recording *Domingo, Carreras, Pavarotti and Mehta in Concert*. This was the recording of an unprecedented worldwide operatic event which took place in Rome on the eve of the 1990 World Cup soccer final. For the first time ever, the almost unbelievable happened. Three tenors, Luciano Pavarotti, José Carreras and Placido Domingo, all megastars in their own right, shared the same stage under the baton of the conductor Zubin Mehta. On the evening of 6 July, the enormous Roman arena called the Baths of Caracalla was filled with a capacity crowd, all eager to hear this amazing concert.

There has always been a healthy competition between them which the media has tried to exaggerate. This exciting and dramatic event, bringing together three major opera stars, was beamed live on television to 54 countries and drew a television audience of more than 1,000 million.

The concert, called the Three Tenors Spectacular, as it came to be known, was organised by the Spanish tenor José Carreras. After having successfully fought off leukaemia which nearly killed him, Carreras founded the José Carreras International Leukaemia Foundation which was to receive money raised by the event. Carreras recalls:

"From the first moment, I thought this could be an event which would be remembered forever. Through the meetings we had beforehand, through the rehearsals, the atmosphere was extraordinary. We had such fun. It was our chance to show how much affection and admiration we have for each other. There is competition between us but in a very sane way, not like in the media. We each keep up our standard and be as good as the next man. Sometimes an artist needs that stimulation. But rivalry? This is wrong."

Still, the media tried their best to find some rumbles of jealousy or sniff out any bad feeling. Journalists speculated in the newspapers about what the atmosphere was really like backstage when the three sang the gala concert. They wondered who decided who would sing first? How would they finish? Which of the three would sing which arias? Pavarotti told reporters how the music was chosen: "Most simple. First Carreras chose, then Domingo, then I." Still the press could hardly believe that Pavarotti allowed his rivals to take a clear run through the range of arias knowing that he would have to sing from what was left over. Pavarotti only roared with laughter: "Me? Only what was left? Listen, I had 'Recondita Armonia', 'Rondine al Nino', 'Sorrento', 'Nessun dorma'. Such arias to be leavings! I tell you there was not one moment of rivalry, of temperament. Soon they will bring out a video of the making of that concert, all the things backstage. Then you see. It was all beautiful."

Despite the scepticism of the journalists, television viewers saw the camaraderie in the wings of the stage. As one tenor left the stage, he met the oncoming tenor with a thump on the back or the sort of clasp one sees football players enjoy when they've scored a goal. The whole event was such a success that there have been rumours of another Three Tenors Spectacular at some time in the future if all three can find the space in their schedules to be available at the same time.

Pavarotti's high profile in The Three Tenors Spectacular merely served to emphasise his ambassadorial role in the vanguard of an overall initiative within the record industry to successfully promote serious music on the same level as pop music. Pavarotti's *Essential* albums paved the way for albums like Nigel Kennedy's recording of Vivaldi's *The Four Seasons* to reach the Pop Charts, and, in their wake, for the major record labels to package and promote the works of all the great composers with the same hi-tech marketing strategy as they promoted Michael Jackson, U2, Dire Straits and Madonna.

PAVAROTTI IN THE PARK

avarotti has referred to himself as a pioneer, always wanting to try new things. In keeping with this characteristic, Pavarotti was the mastermind behind the largest event ever staged in Great Britain, a concert performance in London's Hyde Park, known as Pavarotti in the Park, before an audience of over a quarter of a million. The concert, broadcast live by satellite all over the world was to celebrate Pavarotti's 30th anniversary on the stage as an opera singer. But why share this celebration with Britain? "London is dear to my heart," he said. "I made my first international mark here in 1963 at Covent Garden. It was the real beginning of my real career." So the idea of a concert in Hyde Park was partly as a thank you to the devoted British fans but it was also because Britain is where his first taste of success came from, in Wales with the Rossini chorus.

Pavarotti is always grateful and never forgets. He recalls: "They said if we came in the first 10 it would be amazing. We came first, and at that moment I know I am touching the sky with my finger. Do you know the meaning of this? This Italian expression means to be in contact with God."

It is as if the traditional concert venues are no longer large enough to hold all the people who want to hear him sing. A few years ago in an interview Pavarotti was asked how opera had finally reached so many new people who were never interested in it before and also why he began to perform these gigantic concerts. At the time he replied, "I suppose it is because I love the rapport with human beings. And the sizes of opera houses are so limited . . . And it makes me very, very happy because you are in front of an audience of around 200,000 or more people and you come to a pause in the music and you hear total silence, as if the big arena is empty, that means there is something there, something is happening. That is more wonderful and more moving even than the great roar of applause . . . But I still say we cannot take credit for making opera reach more people. That is the result of television.

"Television has made a huge difference in taking opera back to the people. When television became interested in what opera actually is, it gave everyone with a television set, 100 per cent of the audience, the chance to look at opera and decide if they like it or not. I am sure that for most people it was something completely unexpected and so from two per cent of the television audience twenty years ago, now 20 per cent of those people have begun to be interested in the art form. There are still people who make fun of opera. But now at least they know what it is."

On another occasion, discussing the same subject, Pavarotti did take some credit for bringing opera to new audiences. He said: "I like these big events. It will bring thousands of people who have never been to a classical concert, and that is very important. Of course the music in that environment will never be like singing in Covent Garden. But you do get feedback. You sing a phrase, and then there is a short pause, and you can hear total silence . . . hundreds of thousands of people in total silence. That is amazing."

Pavarotti in the Park was the culmination of the co-operation between the great tenor and every possible benefit that modern technology could possibly offer to make the evening a success. It

cost nearly one million pounds to put on. The concert area
covered 50 acres. Three giant screens around the site were linked
with amplifiers which had to be mounted with cranes. A sound
system powered by the equivalent of 75,000 watts (a household
stereo needs about 50 watts) had to be built to carry the music
over the park. The stage, a 12-metre high replica of a classical
Greek theatre, was designed by Fisher Park, who were also
responsible for staging Madonna, The Rolling Stones and other
major pop events. Twenty metres wide, and weighing 200
tonnes, it took three days to build. An operational crew of 1,000
people were needed. As well as the Philharmonia Orchestra and
Chorus conducted by Pavarotti's friend and colleague Leone
Magiera, there were 12 TV cameras and 15 TV trucks holding
the equipment to record the show. For Pavarotti himself, a
luxury mobile home with an air-purifier and a keyboard was
provided.

Pavarotti sang the concert for free. However, he promised that
£100,000 of the proceeds from the concert would be donated to
the Tree Appeal, headed by the Prince of Wales, who was the
guest of honour at the concert, along with the British Prime
Minister and many other celebrities. The Tree Appeal had been
founded by Prince Charles after Britain's hurricane of 1987 to
replace and replant the thousands of trees that were blown down
in the Royal Parks. The day before the concert Pavarotti planted
a tree in Hyde Park to mark the occasion and was given a silver
spade as a memento.

He then gave a press conference. He looked relaxed, wearing
jeans and a blue cotton safari jacket. However, he shared with
reporters some of his anxieties about the upcoming concert and
gave the world a glimpse of the pressures he has to cope with:
"Tomorrow is a day I would not wish to my worst enemy. It is a
day full of apprehension. I will wake in the morning and I am sure
the voice will not be there. It's always there the day before and the
day after. But never on the day. It's something psychological. I
will try to be free of it. So I will go on all the day thinking am I
going to be good or not? It's the same since my first concert in

1961. But doing live concerts is keeping the doubts in your mind and keeping the freshness of performance."

In the event, the Hyde Park concert was a truly British affair - the skies opened and torrents of rain poured down. However, the British have a welter of experience to fall back on in such circumstances and do not wilt under the extremes of weather and over 100,000 people, draped in various swathes of plastic sheeting, and even bin bags, turned out for the concert. It would have taken more than a downpour to keep them away. They sat in the park in the pouring rain for one and half hours and by all accounts enjoyed themselves enormously. The rain drenched everyone equally - The Prince and Princess of Wales, the Prime Minister, celebrities and the estimated 125,000 crowd that had actually turned out for the event. The rain failed, however, to quench their emotions and their gratitude. Nor did it drown Pavarotti's taste for outdoor concerts. To mark the 500th anniversary of the year of the arrival of Columbus in America, he will sing in two concert performances of *Aïda* in New York City's Central Park.

STAYING AT
THE TOP

Pavarotti, now in his mid-fifties, shows no sign of vocal wear and tear. In fact, by all accounts the great voice is in great shape. However, the stakes rise ever higher and higher as the audiences increase exponentially and technology brings the listener ever closer and closer to the most minute nuance of Pavarotti's voice. Some opera houses have booked Pavarotti three years ahead. His recording company have booked him up with recordings as far ahead as the millenium. Pavarotti divides up his year into two. In the first half he sings primarily in Europe. July is the month reserved for rest, usually spent in his summer home in Pesaro on the Adriatic coast. The second half of the year, September to December, he lives in his flat in New York City and performs his engagements in America. Every New Year's Eve he does a special concert in different venues all over the world.

How does Pavarotti deal with the extraordinary pressure of being Pavarotti? One rule he follows is never to perform more than 50 or 60 times a year. He has never let himself be swallowed up by show business. Pavarotti is older than his nearest 'rivals' but his voice is in top condition. He only sings what is right for his voice.

But there are other sides to Pavarotti, other sources of inner strength which help cope with life at the top. Pavarotti has a private passion for horses. He owns them, adores them and sings to them. Pavarotti's horse hobby provides a release from the remorseless attention that follows his every step in the opera world, during the many months of the year that he spends on the road. He has even promoted a four-day Pavarotti International Horseshow where some of the world's finest showjumping horses performed on Pavarotti's extensive acres in Modena. The show was so successful that it is to become a permanent yearly fixture on the international showjumping circuit. It will continue to commemorate Pavarotti's love of horses for generations to come. And whether Modena likes it or not, its native son has brought home even more world fame, this time on its very doorstep.

Pavarotti's infatuation with horses has been a part of him longer than music. He says: "I fell in love with them when I was a boy on my uncle's farm. I rode them all the time and I rode them as a man when I returned here from my tours. I made efforts to ride them whenever I was singing abroad.

"You know, I have kept a record of the best 78 horses I have ridden anywhere in the world. I have them all in a notebook, like a boy who writes down football scores."

Does Pavarotti still climb into the saddle on occasion? He seemed hesitant about answering the question, but finally confessed: "Two years ago, my favourite horse died. She was an Irish mare called Vagabond. I have never ridden since and I shall not ride again."

Referring to the showjumping event which bears his name Pavarotti said: "What you see today is only the beginning." Pavarotti may no longer ride himself but he has found other ways to perpetuate and renew his affair with the horse.

PAVAROTTI THE PAINTER

There is another more solitary hobby which imparts some balance into the hectic rush of his singing life and provides an inner pool of creative energy from which he can draw resources. Any spare moments which Pavarotti is able to find are devoted to his paintbrush and canvas. "I love painting so much I can't eat," he declared. During a long night of insomnia some years ago, Pavarotti was suddenly seized with the urge to paint, to create something with paint: "I picked up paints and brushes and exploited my unexplainable mania," he said, "I painted for nine hours without stopping, feeling an indescribable joy. I love vibrant colours. My paintings give me immense satisfaction the way music gives me pleasure. I am able to relive unforgettable moments." Subsequently, he has even told the press: "Painting sometimes gives me greater satisfaction than singing. Since I was a small boy in Modena, I have longed for brush and canvas." Pavarotti now paints every day. He paints in a bold, simple, child-like style.

"I am so impassioned by painting, I feel forced to spend every free minute with my brushes in my hand," Pavarotti told journalists. Recently he held an exhibition of 50 of his paintings and original silk screen prints. Painting, like Pavarotti's horse hobby, relaxes him and provides him with some serenity: "I pass hours and whole days closed in my hotel room, immersed in this work. I don't feel tired or hungry or tense. I often forget to eat."

Pavarotti pursues his hobby with all the dedication of an art student. He studies the paintings of the Masters, visiting museums, churches and galleries whenever he is away on tour. Villages in Italy, towns nestled into mountaintops, ships, harbours, houses, gondolas and seascapes have all found their way onto Pavarotti's canvas. One of the subjects Pavarotti loves to paint, as well as eat, is asparagus. He has even painted one of his favourite desserts: tricolour melon balls, poached in Cointreau with French vanilla ice cream.

Pavarotti explains the philosophical side of his passion for painting: "I'm an extrovert, I love people. I love music, I don't have a fitness schedule to keep me energised," he says, "and I don't worry about tomorrow."

"Painting is an obsession like anything else. This strange and curious experience has left me relaxed and serene. When I finish a canvas, I feel I have created the world."

THE GLASGOW DIET
AND CONCERT

arly in 1992, Pavarotti went on one of his strictest diet
régimes yet. While dismissing media claims that his
rumoured weight of 22 stone was threatening his future
career, he had been warned that, by continuing to carry
such a bulk, he was at risk from heart problems and infections.
His mobility on stage was also starting to be affected.

Arriving in Scotland in late February 1992 to prepare for a
sold-out concert at the Scottish Exhibition Centre on March 5, he
announced to the world that he was taking advantage of the
seclusion of his exclusive hotel to go on a strict diet. He revealed
his diet plans at a press conference in which reporters were kept
at a distance by a line of white tape on the floor to avoid trans-
mitting any cold germs or throat infections.

"If you see me four weeks from now, I will have a red carna-
tion - or you will never recognise me," he said, announcing that
he had already lost eight pounds and predicting a further loss of
25lb in as many days. The hotel's executive chef, responsible for
Pavarotti's diet while he was staying there, said: "He's very easy
to look after. His request was that all the food we prepared had to
be simple and fresh, with very little spice." The official Pavarotti

menu at the hotel consisted of salad, fruit, cheese and yoghurt, but leaked reports from Luciano's suite included sightings of pasta and marzipan-topped cake.

The concert in Glasgow was a true Pavarotti spectacular. The exhibition hall, as large as an aircraft hangar, had been specially enlarged by an extra block of seats to hold more than 8,500 fans, some of whom had paid up to £450 for a ticket. As at Hyde Park, Pavarotti used skilfully-placed microphones to get the maximum sound penetration, assisted by a virtuoso sound engineer from Pavarotti's recording company.

The programme he sang was a very full one, dispelling speculation about health problems affecting his ability to perform and proving that, at 57, his voice was as magnificent and as moving as ever - that the old Luciano was still there. Arias sung that night ranged from 'Recondita armonia' from *Tosca* through to 'Dio ti giocondi, o sposa' from *Otello*, now firmly in his repertoire, and prompting critics and fans to long for a London *Otello* at the Royal Opera House. The concert finished with six encores, the last of which was, of course, 'Nessun Dorma' - by now the Luciano Pavarotti signature tune.

CHEVALIER, AND
FUTURE PLANS

In April 1992, Pavarotti was presented with the Légion d'Honneur medal by the French Foreign Minister, Roland Dumas, at the Bastille Opera. This was a fitting tribute to an operatic legend and champion of art who has now brought the gift of opera to millions world wide - many of whom might have never known what an aria was, or have been bothered to find out.

Pavarotti remains booked up solidly for many years to come. One exciting future plan is to stage another "Three Tenors" concert with Placido Domingo and José Carreras, probably in Japan in 1994. Speaking in Cannes, Carreras revealed: "It is just a project at this stage, but I hope we can be together for early 1994. If we do it too often it would lose some of its magic - but at the moment, we absolutely want to be together again."

RETIREMENT

This is a very sad subject to consider, even as Pavarotti continues to climb higher and higher. But it is on his mind. He is only too aware of how impermanent the human voice is. He said: "You know, there are great similarities between the careers of a singer and a horse. Some jumping horses go on till they get to 20 years old. For others, they get to 12 and suddenly they are finished. No one can tell when it is going to happen.

"The human voice is equally unpredictable. Every day I wonder, will I have one year more, or two, or three, or ten? I love, I adore music. I still enjoy travelling the world. But I know it must end. And when it does there will be this . . ."

What Pavarotti refers to by "this . . ." is his showjumping event, and his horses, which he plans to become much more involved with when he does, eventually, retire.

Pavarotti spoke candidly with Nicolas Soames of London's *Daily Telegraph* about Joan Sutherland's retirement, and it is perhaps here that we can gain some further insights into his own feelings on the matter.

"This has been very sad for me," he said. "Joan has been an

incredible colleague and we have done so many things . . . I know that we singers tend to stop two or three years too late, although in the case of Joan I think she stopped a couple of years too early. I am not thinking of retirement - Otello has recharged my batteries and in any case I will find it very difficult to live without music, without the theatre. It is what my personality needs."

"When people ask me if I like the applause, I say 'Of course I do'. People who say it is terrible not being able to walk down the street without being recognised . . . it is not true. Believe me, it is not unpleasant!"

Not unpleasant indeed! What will Pavarotti, a man who obviously enjoys being a celebrity, do next? He has sung all over the world, in every major theatre, he has packed huge venues and sold millions of albums. His amazing voice is immortalised for all time using the highest-quality equipment - an advantage that Caruso and Gigli didn't have. In a world where Andy Warhol promised everyone 15 minutes of fame, Pavarotti has remained a household word for years. The future still looks bright for the baker's son from Modena.